ANTHONY TAYLOR

Tips from Top

The Secrets of How to Navigate Middle Management

*For my Mum, Nina Taylor, you helped me believe I could achieve anything
I wanted, if I was willing to put the work in.
I miss you.*

*For Jo, you gave me the love and support
to help make that happen. For that I'm eternally grateful.
I love you.*

Contents

Foreword

How can reading Tips from the Top – the secrets of how to navigate middle management help me in my career to be a better leader?

That's the question I want you to remember and reflect on as you read this book.

What Anthony has done, with the help of the many fantastic contributors he has managed to assemble, is provide you with a star chart to help you navigate your career whatever the weather.

The sheer breadth of experience that all 28 contributors bring, ensures that there is a wealth of information everyone can take from this book. Whether you are a rising star in an SME or a seasoned veteran of a multi-national, there is wisdom on every page that you can use to navigate your career.

That they candidly share some of their mistakes alongside their best achievements, is both heartening and rewarding in equal measure. It shows that career success is not down to some celestial quality reserved only for a chosen few, but within the grasp of every single one of us.

Each of you will take different things from the book which is why at the end of each chapter Anthony has posed two questions for you to reflect on. The true value of this book to you, will be in how much time and effort you are willing to put in to reflect on these and to then do something different.

The map may show you the way but you've got to put the work in to get to the destination. This is not a book to read and put down, but rather to re-read until it's well thumbed over years of use.

To get the best out of other people, you have to get best out of yourself. This book will help with that.

Nigel Risner

Chief Zoo Keeper

Business Speaker Of The Year

Communications Expert and Motivational Speaker

Author of: It's a Zoo Around Here; Zoo Keeper Rules for the Office; The Impact Code

Preface

The idea for this book came to me while listening to a professional speaker on goal setting. I got excited by it for a few hours then cooled on it. However, over the next few weeks the idea wouldn't go away. During that time, I reflected on how my career had progressed. When it had gone well, when not so well.

I also remember the difference it made when I worked for a fantastic organisation with a great culture, compared to one where the culture did not fit my personal values. I have had the privilege to work for some fantastic people. People who inspired me, pushed me, coached me, mentored me. Who gave me confidence and built me up. I was also inspired by Ricardo Semler and his book Maverick! very early in my career which put me on the path for the kind of leader I wanted to be.

I also worked for some who had the opposite effect. The 'Leadershits' I call them. The bullies, micro-managers and credit-thieves. You know the type. Maybe you've worked for some of them too. I remember the difference they made to me and the effect that had on me at work and at home.

Aged 40, I decided to change career and spend my time working with managers at all levels, building their leadership capital and improving their performance and mental fitness. I've always been fascinated about what it is that the world's best, in any aspect of life, do that separates them from the rest of us. I believe we can learn a lot from them.

Selfishly, I also wanted to understand why I never made it to the top. To find explanations for some of the things that happened in my career and unpick some of the mistakes I made. Clue, it was never about technical ability.

So, I decided to ask. I initially approached some of the people who had led me in my career and some others I'd come across and respected greatly. I then asked them for their recommendations and expanded my search across the globe.

What I found was that people were incredibly willing to share their time and knowledge with me for the benefit of you the reader. This means that I've been able to compile a collection of insights and experience of 28 people from across the world. People who have risen to the top in their respective fields. CEOs, Directors, authors, thought leaders and successful entrepreneurs. They have led and are leading companies like Starbucks UK, SainsburysArgos, Disney, Rentokil, Costcutter, Rymans and many more.

Their collective experience can be measured in hundreds of years. The wisdom they've shared, priceless.

My hope is that this book will help you in your career. To achieve the things you want to achieve and more importantly to be a great manager and leader. One that inspires and builds up others, who makes a positive difference and is remembered for it.

We spend so much of our lives at work, with people we have little or no choice about. I think it's a tragedy that so many of us have a miserable time because of poor management and leadership skills. It doesn't have to be this way.

This book is my small contribution in helping to change that. I hope you enjoy it and find it useful in realising your potential and helping other achieve theirs.

How to use the book

My intention with this book is that you will use it as a learning and development tool. Therefore, after each contribution you'll find two questions:

- What two things have struck you most from what was said?
- What one thing will you do differently as a result of what you've learnt from this chapter?

There is space to make notes on any thoughts and insights you have. You could just choose to read it and put it down, but we learn better when we have chance to reflect.

Of course, knowledge without application is useless. If we don't do something different as a result, then nothing will change. Hence the second question. Read, reflect, implement, reflect, re-implement. Repeat.

I'd like nothing more than to know it's being used this way, so please feel free to email me a picture of your thoughts and commitments from a chapter that's resonated with you. You can find my email address at the back of the book.

Who this book is for?

This book is for anyone in 'middle management'. I don't normally like labels. Sure, they have a purpose and can in the right context be extremely helpful. In some contexts, less so. It's very difficult to get an accurate comparison between job roles based solely on job titles. A marketing manager in a global firm might have a budget in the tens of millions and responsibility for lots of people. The same person in an SME might have a budget of £100K and only one person to lead.

So, for the purpose of this book my definition of 'middle management' is anyone from a first line manager to someone directly under C-suite. Whatever level you are at and whatever level you aspire to be, there will be things you can learn from the people and pages within.

It's not all about trying to reach the top either. Only a very small percentage will and many of us just don't have the interest to even try - and that's OK. This book will help you be the best leader you can be. As a manager and leader, you have the power to affect people's lives, for better or for worse. I hope the wisdom shared by the people I interviewed will help you make it for the better.

Good luck in your career and have fun.

Acknowledgement

I'd first and foremost like to thank all the people I interviewed for this book. Without their time, enthusiasm and willingness to share their thoughts and experiences there would not be a book.

I'd also like to thank some of those very people for their encouragement along the way in particular Damian Hughes, Ken Perry and Peter Freeth. My book cover designer Andy Meaden for doing such a great job and Joanna Penn for her fantastic podcast, books and website on self-publishing.

Thanks should also go to my family who have always supported me through thick and thin and never once doubted me, especially my father Dr. Andrew Taylor. You have been the embodiment of every positive quality identified in this book and without your love and support, especially over the last decade, I would not have been able to do what I have. Thank you.

To my kids, Beth, Jess, Will and Merryn who have heard me talk about this project for two years.

I'd also like to thank my closest friends for their support and much needed cajoling at times to get it finished; Anthony, John, Ben, Andy, Paul and Dom. Thanks fellas.

1

The Questions

The Ten Questions

After deciding to go ahead with the book I spent a lot of time kicking around how I'd approach interviewing each person. What questions would I ask? Would I ask everyone the same ones or just a few to start off and then go with the flow?

I came up with a list of more than 20 at first and then decided that this would be too many. I was also worried that if I just went with the flow with each interview that I could be biased by my own interests and whims.

On the other hand if I went with the same questions for everyone, the end result could be too narrow and the variety of responses too limited.

Despite these concerns that's the route I opted to take. I was very quickly reassured that my fears were unfounded and that the variety of depth content of responses would not disappoint.

Some contributors have chosen to keep their responses brief, yet no less insightful. What I think works as a result, is the variety which creates a nice change of pace when reading the book.

In the end I narrowed it down to ten questions, which are:

- *What was your best memory or achievement as a middle manager?*
- *Who was the best boss you ever had and why?*
- *What was the greatest challenge you faced as a middle manager?*

- *What was the biggest mistake you made when you were a middle manager?*
- *What personal qualities do you see in the best middle managers?*
- *What skills do you think middle managers should focus on developing to ensure their effectiveness over their career?*
- *What do you know now that you wish you knew as a middle manager?*
- *What's your one 'Tip for the Top'?*
- *What is the one book you'd recommend to every middle manager?*
- *What question haven't I asked that you think I should have?*

Enjoy the rest of the book and the variety of fascinating answers that came from just ten simple questions.

2

Damian Hughes

Consultant & Visiting Professor of Organisational Psychology and Change, Manchester Metropolitan University; Author of The Winning Mindset

Damian Hughes wears a few different hats. He is the Professor of Organisational Psychology and Change, at Manchester Metropolitan University for one. He is also a sought after consultant, working across a whole range of different organisations in education, business and sport; creating high performing cultures.

His sporting clients include the Scottish Rugby Union, England Rugby League, England Roses netball team, Leeds Rhinos, Warrington Wolves and Canberra Raiders rugby league sides

He is also author of a number of books including The Barcelona Way, The Five Steps to a Winning Mindset, How to think like Alex Ferguson, Liquid Thinking, Liquid Leadership, Change Inspiration and many more. He lives in Sale, Manchester.

What was your best memory or achievement as a middle manager?

I think my best achievement was taking over as the HR director for the Port Sunlight Plant, for Unilever. Now, to give some context, the Lever brothers started at Port Sunlight, so Lord Leverhulme set up the place and it's a heritage site now. This place itself always reminded me of the Truman Show, where the houses can only be maintained in a certain way and things like that; but the factory lies at the heart of it.

And when I went in there, in the early 2000s; the performance had declined, a lot of complacency set in. Many Eastern European factories were starting to overtake it in terms of its measures. And my brief was to go in and look at two options, whether we needed to reduce the size or whether we could get it back up to an operational level.

So for the next two and half years we did an awful lot of just introducing the principles of high performance, and getting people to understand the psychology of change. And there's a whole heap of different stories I could tell you.

We ended up having Daley Thompson come and work on the factory lines with our guys; we had the captain of the Brazil 1970 world cup team, Carlos Alberto, spend time with us. I wrote the book, Liquid Thinking, about some of the experiences of it.

So, it was a really rich learning ground, but what we did was turn the performance around. We went from the bottom quartile, to the top three factories in Europe, while keeping a lot of the same staff, but just getting them to understand a lot of the principles of change.

The nice thing is, and I suppose this is why I mention it; the legacy continues where I still keep in touch with a lot of the guys. I left 14 years ago, and there's some of them that still keep in touch with me. A lot of them are still employing some of the principles that we taught them at the very early stage; so, it just felt like an opportunity to shape lives, as well as shape the business.

I know it's easy to look back with rose-tinted specs. I hated it for the first, eight months! It was a slog, but once I made the mindset shift myself, to actually say, "Come on, this is worth investing time and doing", it became fun.

That was really special for me.

Who was the best boss you ever had and why?

I was the sort of lad that if you went to my teachers at school and asked, "What was he like as a lad?" They'd have said, "He was a nice lad but he was a bit of a pain." And I wasn't malicious or malevolent in my intent. I just got bored easily, and when I get bored, I sort of try and disrupt things.

And I was very much like that at work. So, I think managing me, would be a nightmare. Because of the sort of character that I am. I had one man, when I first went into the corporate world; a real gentleman, called Alan Walters, that took me under his wing a little bit and tried to guide me past some of the corporate potholes that I was driving into. Only because I just didn't understand what I was doing.

There's a story I sometimes think about where, I told my mum that I was going to be a football coach at Manchester United and she said, "Well what are you going to do when you get found out?"

Because she knew I didn't know what I was doing. And I always had that sort of mindset, that I always kept waiting to get found out.

Which meant that when Alan Walters, would phone me up and say, "Oh, I need to see you tomorrow," I genuinely used to go in and expect that I was going to get handed my notice.

He didn't, what he did do was to invest a lot of time to try and polish some of the rougher edges, that I had. Sadly, he passed away four years ago. I'd left by this stage but even after he had died, I wrote his wife a letter. I wanted to share with her the impact that he'd had on my life, because I regard him as a really significant character and influence on my life and career.

I knew how little I knew; and the only thing that I could say with any certainty was that I really had no clue what I was doing at that point.

But I was prepared to work, I was prepared to listen, I was prepared to try my best at whatever I was asked. When you're clear about who you are, and you don't try and puff it up with ego and things like that, there's always people like Alan Walters in most workplaces that are prepared to just help you and guide you.

What was the greatest challenge you faced as a middle manager?

Just conformity.

As I said before if you had spoken to my teachers, they'd have said that I was nice lad, I just didn't conform so much. Conformity was a big challenge for me, that and I struggled to be diplomatic at times.

When I would see things going on that I either didn't understand, or felt were a case of people trying to build up their ego, or empire building rather than doing things for the corporate good. I really struggled with that.

I struggled with viewing people as numbers on a spreadsheet, rather than seeing the human beings behind it, and the collateral damage as a result of the decisions being made. So, I really struggled with that conformity to sometimes sit there.

The other one I struggled with, and it might sound a little bit silly to people reading this, was, just being sat in meetings. I struggled to sit still. When I first started in the corporate world, I used to find it bizarre the amount of meetings people would have. Someone might even have a meeting to discuss a meeting.

It's not something that I ever really came to terms with. Just the amount of meetings, and the amount of people just sat round talking rather than doing. I really used to struggle with that and I now regard it as a badge of honour!

In our world now, many people are self-employed so I'll ask them, "At what stage did you become unemployable?" And sometimes they'll reply: "Oh no, I might still go back," and I realise they are not quite there yet. But then other people, will say: "Oh yeah, I passed that when I was within a year of doing what we do."

What was the biggest mistake you made when you were a middle manager?

I made so many of them. I could probably share with you a few, that might be useful.

One was that I was rubbish at building consensus, so I had the view that I would ask for forgiveness, not permission. So I do something, and then think, I'll justify it afterwards. Or if my intent is good, I'll just get on and do it. So, I would describe myself as driven to take action, and then see how things went. And if it didn't work, come back and learn from it quickly.

But I understand that, I could have made life a lot easier for myself by just trying to build consensus. Partly it was my lack of conformity. And this isn't making excuses, but part of it was I just lacked patience, to do things like that. So, as a middle manager, you need to build consensus; you need to manage upwards, as well as downwards. I was dreadful at doing that.

I'll give you a really good example of it, which sounds funny, but ended up being quite serious in terms of my job.

One of the things that we did at Port Sunlight, was to invest a lot of the budget in terms of training and development for our people. The message we were giving was, "We're not going to reward you financially, but if you're prepared to go the extra mile and show some aptitude to want to improve things, we will give you access to opportunities to improve them."

And one of the things I tried to do was to expand their frame of reference, because it was quite an insular world. So, I called on a lot of favours from people, from my own contacts, mainly in sport, to come in and speak to the guys in the factory. The idea was to share some of their insights about high performance.

My dad was a boxing coach, he came in a couple of times and he brought some of his world champion boxers that he trained. We did different things like getting in local people that had raised lots of money for charity in the local community, to talk about how they'd done it.

The long story short, I ended up pulling in a favour where we got Daley Thompson to come and spend the day working in the factory. I called in another favour and Carlos Alberto came in. So, the people in the factory loved it, and used to come to us and say, "Who's next month? Who's next month?"

And in the spirit of developing responsibility I said to them, "You should start sorting it out."

So what I use to do is write letters to people like the Pope, or to the American Presidents and invite them to come in. And the idea was you get a rejection letter off them, and would put those letters up there on a wall and say, "We're still aiming big." It became like a real theme. But when the lads used to say, "Oh, who's coming in next?" I'd say, "You try and sort out who's coming in. Don't keep asking me."

They started taking responsibility to do things that appealed to their interests. We had Sir Garfield Sobers come in, which one of the lads had arranged. Then long story short, one guy said, "I'd love to see Nick Leeson come in." He was the guy who brought down Barings Bank.

So I said to him, "Well, you sort out it out then," and then thought no more of it.

Six months later, this lad came in with a pile of letters, between him and Nick Leeson who was living out in Galway. This lad had tracked him down. And he couldn't read or write properly, the lad in the factory; but he'd got his girlfriend to write to him.

It ended up with Nick Leeson coming back and saying he'd do it, but I needed to phone him up to confirm it. I'll be honest, I was reluctant to do this, but equally there was a point that I'd set them this challenge and he had gone ahead and done it, so we need to reward it.

So, I spoke to Nick on the phone and he said, "Listen, I understand the sort of implications of using my name, but I'm going to talk about keeping things under control, not letting things spiral." So, I thought, "Well that's an angle we can justify." So we signed him up to come in on one particular day.

Now another thing I used to do was phone up the local press and invite them to come into these sessions. On the understanding that when the photographer came in, he would always take pictures of our own staff. And the idea behind that was, these lads would go in the pub of an evening, and their mates in the pub would say, "Oh, I saw you, in the paper today with

Daley Thompson." So suddenly, they took real pride in the workplace, and when their peer group were saying, "Your place sounds brilliant!" It started to generate this momentum.

One of the local reporters asked me, "Who's next month?" so I told him that it was Nick Leeson from Barings Bank. He just replied; "Oh right great, I'll come along." The local newspapers then ran, this story, on page 3, suggesting I was bringing in a rogue trader, and the article was all about the negative implications of what Nick Leeson was going to teach our staff.

There were also some quotes attributed to me that I hadn't made. As is often the case, the national papers then picked up the local paper's story and ended up running it. The outcome was a range of bad publicity, with me right in the eye of it.

I genuinely thought I was going to be dismissed, at one stage, because of the implications of what was going on. Everyone was getting involved, from the Unilever head office press people to the chairman.

In the end, it goes back to that first point I said about, just being clearer about who you are and what you stand for. I accepted I'd made a mistake, but I done it with positive intention. I tried to make things happen, and I think that was the thing that saved me. The fact that I could show there was a consistency to what I'd done and a genuine good reason behind it. This was a pretty big mistake, but there was a consistency that I was doing it for the right reasons. It was the only thing that saved me.

What is the one book you'd recommend to every middle manager?

When I was at Port Sunlight, I was looking for a book about change, like a manual for going through it. In the end I couldn't find anything I felt fitted the bill. I wanted to give the lads a manual, for them to take to their teams and their families and the football teams we were running.

If it was too academic, they wouldn't read it. If it was too light, and sort of effeminate or something like this, they wouldn't read that either; they'd dismiss it with cynicism. I couldn't find anything that fit the bill so I decided to write it myself.

It ended up being the very first book I wrote called Liquid Thinking. I wanted to try and write a book that was about the psychology of high performance, but accessible.

And I made a list of people like Richard Branson and Muhammad Ali that I wanted to interview and I was lucky enough to be able to go and do that with them. But even when I written it, I still thought, "They would still dismiss it," so if you said to them this is Richard Branson, and this is how he built Virgin," they'd say, "Richard Branson's mum and dad were rich." Or, if you said Muhammad Ali, they'd say, "Yeah, but he was naturally talented."

So I didn't want to give them an excuse, so what I decided to do was feature in between the chapters, stories of lads that work in the factory. So there was stories of a guy that had built his own house, to get his kids in to the best school.

There was a story of a guy that had built a canal boat, where he planned to spend his retirement. There was a rally and motocross champion in the factory; and I interviewed them about their stories, and featured them in the book. And the idea was to show them how their mindset was exactly the same as Branson's, just the challenges were different.

Or, Muhammad Ali winning the world title was the same as the guy winning the rally motocross title. And that was the idea behind the book. And so we gave it to every member of our staff, that worked there, to show them that choosing your mindset is accessible to everybody. Talent, was maybe a differentiator, or our starting position in life may have been different; but in terms of the mindset to embrace change and take challenges on, was always the same.

So even the Nick Leeson story had a learning point, which was that we did what we thought was right at the time, for the right reasons.

What we were trying to do is to instil a "can-do" attitude, in them; and I think that was sometimes at odds with the wider organisation. I see it now that I've left the corporate world, I see it a lot where people say, "Oh, we value innovation," and yet innovation is sometimes getting things wrong. What I see is they don't like the messiness of getting things wrong, but they tell you they value innovation. Those two ideas are counterproductive. You can't have innovation without cock-ups.

What personal qualities do you see in the best middle managers?

Well, there's a couple of things here. I think one is the **ability to listen**.

Middle managers are in a unique position, they need to listen and then be able to translate. So, I think the listen bit is very important. It's such a quiet quality it often gets missed. But, I see it as being essential; you have to be able to listen both to members of your team that want to come and just talk to you, and then from your senior managers too and become the translator in both directions.

The second quality is, I think, about developing a level of **kindness**.

Kindness relates to yourself, because I think it's probably the position where you see the squeeze really happens. You're constantly under pressure, there's demands that are always shifting, that are moving at a fair pace.

First of all, the ability to be kind to yourself, in that position. There will always be things that you either can't do, or you just don't have the time or the capacity to do anything about. So being kind rather than beating yourself up is the starting point. And then when you start doing that for yourself, you start recognising the kindness in others. As a result it's easier to start being kind towards others.

Middle management is often seen as an abject lesson in frustration; people haven't done exactly what you want, how you want it. Or senior management haven't listened; things like that.

When you come at the world from a kind lens, you often see that people are fighting the wrong battles in the best way that they can.

I just see it lacking so much in lots of different worlds, including the corporate world as well. It just seems to be relentless. When I go and peer into that world now, I see the pace of it, I see the demands that people are under, I see the sacrifices that people are making. Both on their health and their family time.

What skills do you think middle managers should focus on developing to ensure their effectiveness over their career?

Skills are going to change. I think change is essential. There's a lovely quote that I heard during an interview recently. The person was the Director of Barcelona Football Club; and he said, "Your talent will get you in the dressing room, your behaviours will decide whether we keep you there or not."

It's such a powerful quote, in that talent is almost a prerequisite, so it doesn't matter what industry you're in. Your ability to do the job, is almost presupposed by the fact that you're doing the job.

What I mean about behaviours is dealing with change. Because that will be constant. The demands for the job are already there, but your ability to deal with change, to be able to cope with it, to be able to understand it, to coach people with it, to understand how you respond under pressure, what are your key triggers about how you do it.

All of that, it's emotional intelligence. All of these factors are going to be essential, in the changing world. People say that the jobs of ten years' time haven't been invented yet; or that kids leaving school will be doing jobs that haven't been invented yet. The pace of that change is going to be relentless.

Our psychology isn't evolving nearly as fast, so we need to understand how our brains cope with pressure, how we respond to it. How we deal with change and all of that is probably the most essential skill of middle managers.

I remember talking to a young athlete, he was on one of the teams I work with; and I said to him,

"Are you planning a two-year career or a twenty-year career?" "What do you mean?" he replied.

I said, "Well if it's two years, carry on with the pace you're doing. Carry on beating yourself up. Carry on with the relentlessness of what you're doing; because, I'm sure you'll be successful for about two years. But if you're planning a twenty year career, I think your behaviours will need to be different. You would be a bit kinder to yourself. You would accept mistakes a bit easier.

That principle applies in other jobs too. If you are in sales and want a two-year career, then carry on being ruthless. Carry on being snide and underhand:

And you'll be successful for about two years. If it's a twenty years career you want, then you don't be.

What do you know now that you wish you knew as a middle manager?

Don't take your own welfare for granted. I think, one of the big lessons that I learnt was I thought the job mattered more than it did. And what I mean by that is that when I went to Port Sunlight, I threw myself into it. I had a really tough first eight months when I wasn't sure whether I wanted to do it; and then I made a commitment that, I was going to throw myself in.

And then, for the next two years or so, I was relentless, I pushed myself, and I really thought it mattered. I ended up contracting meningitis, so the welfare question became relevant, and it was my own fault.

I'd run myself into the ground. I allowed myself to get rundown and then become open to an illness, and unfortunately for me it was meningitis. And it knocked me out for quite a while. I remember, my wife told me this a long time afterwards, that when she told me bosses that I was seriously ill, the first question they asked was, "Is it contagious? Do we need to shut the site down?"

It took them another twenty-four hours to phone back to find out how I actually was.

When she told me I initially felt a bit affronted by it, "How dare they do that?" I thought.

But then after a while I realised, it was my mistake not theirs. I had allowed them to take my welfare for granted. This was the learning I took from that.

I thought, I mattered. And the reality was, I was a bit of a number and as long as I was a doing a good job, then that was great. I'd misunderstood the psychological contract; they'd never changed, my job was just to come in and do the job. I then started applying a meaning to it that wasn't there. It was a meaning for my benefit. It was my self-esteem. My ego that kicked in; that made me keep going back and thinking that I was really important.

So, they never changed, I did. And I misunderstood the 'psychological contract' between employer and employee. I forgot that I was a number. If I'd have died that day when I had meningitis; I've no doubt they'd have expressed sympathy for a day or two, but then very quickly they'd would have said, "We need to get someone else in to carry on the production."

And they'd be able to change with that. They never promised to do anything other than that. It was me that misunderstood it and applied a meaning that wasn't there. What I often say is, I mentally resigned that day. Although it took me another two years to physically follow through with my resignation.

But, it was a catalyst for the thoughts that I'd had, that I outline here. I didn't think the corporate world was a domain where I could flourish. I always thought I was going to struggle too much, in terms of the lack of conformity. It was always going to inhibit me in some way, and that lack of diplomacy. Asking for forgiveness and not permission. Some of those principles that we touched on here, weren't ever going to lead to a long career in the corporate world, so I realised that I needed to start moving on and that was the catalyst for me; I realised I had misunderstood the 'psychological contract'.

They hadn't changed, just me. I've never felt bitter to them, because they were always consistent.

In some ways I'm glad I didn't come to that realisation before, because if I had of done, I think they'd have bought my head and not my heart. I would have been a bit more logical and pragmatic about it.

I'm glad I didn't because of the richness of the experiences that I had and some of the contacts that I still have now. It brought me some great benefits, but too much of it tipped me over the edge and wasn't helpful for me.

What's your one Tip for the Top?

Courage. It's a small word but there's a huge implication behind it. In my case it was the courage to not conform, and to stay true to myself. That's how I would apply it to me.

But for other people it might be the courage to persevere with an idea they've got. It might be the courage to put your hand up in a meeting and share a thought, or to disagree with something when you see group-think going on. It might be the courage to say no to your bosses, because you want to get away to your children's Christmas concert, or whatever it is. It's the courage not just to follow what everybody else is doing.

We're pack animals. The power of the pack can be strong. We want to fit in. We want to do what other people do. And I think, it's too easy to go with the herd, and intuitively know, "This isn't the right thing for me. I disagree with this."

I think having the courage to sometimes step away from that, is a really powerful quality. First of all, it can be developed; but, the first thing is, just to recognise it, as a quality.

What question haven't I asked that you think I should have?

What a brilliant question, just to think about.

I think a really good question that I'm often intrigued about is 'Who sowed your golden seed? Who was the person that saw a potential in you, long before you did?'

It was Sigmund Freud that said we all need somebody that sows the golden seed. At some stage in our life we all need somebody, whether it's a parent, a grandparent or an uncle. We need somebody in our life that believes in us long before we believe in ourselves; that sees a potential, that lies untapped.

And I think, that's often a really brilliant question to ask somebody about:

For me there are a few. I was lucky, in terms of, both my Mum and Dad. I'd say it was my Dad in lots of ways, because he left school at 14, with no education. He was a bastard child in post-war Manchester. A real Catholic family, where that would be a significant burden to carry. He ended up setting up a boxing gym and he trained quite a few world champions. He taught himself to read and write and wrote a number of books. I think he was the one, that always sowed that seed of being true to yourself.

I was lucky enough with the teachers too. People like Bernard Counsell who I know taught your Dad, Andrew. When I went to him, I'd been expelled for fighting and being too disruptive and he and a teacher called, Peter Wood, went and spoke up for me.

And so my expulsion got downgraded to a suspension. And they sort of took me under their wing and sort of tried to say, "You don't need to be at war with the world, there's other ways of doing this."

Which, again, you don't necessarily appreciate at the time, but as an adult, you can look back and just recognise, they didn't have to do that. There was nothing in it for them to do it. They could have turned a blind eye.

So, I've been lucky, I feel I've had a number of people that have done that.

What two things have struck you most from what was said?

What one thing will you do differently as a result of what you've learnt from this chapter?

3

Darcy Willson-Rymer

CHIEF EXECUTIVE OFFICER OF COST CUTTER SUPERMARKET GROUPS

Darcy Willson-Rymer is the chief executive officer of Cost Cutter Supermarket Groups, a chain of 1500 convenient stores up and down the country. He has been in retail and services all of his life. Darcy was with Young Brands for 19 years, the owners of the Pizza Hut and KFC chains. He started with them as a waiter in 1984 and worked his way up and left that business as a senior director.

Darcy spent three years with Unilever and he built a clothes care company called Personal Service. Following that he worked for Starbucks for five years, going from regional vice president for Europe to managing director for the UK and Ireland.

What was your best memory or achievement as a middle manager?

Pizza Hut, when I had been an area manager for about a year. It was classic middle management. I'd been in the job a year, and had won an award ahead of a significant number of older, longer serving peers. That was kind of a bit of a surprise and a shock. It was a good piece of recognition that was based on the approach that I took to team leadership of my area at the time.

Effectively, the approach was simple. I was in a new part of the business, when Pizza Hut delivery had just started up, so it was relatively new, and pretty much seen as the poor relation and the underdog of the business at the time.

We were pretty much taking a head down customer first approach, a "so here's what we must do in order to satisfy customers".

I decided to approach leading the team with a great humility.

Rather than assuming we're the best at everything, we decided to learn from other parts of the organization, but executing it perfectly, and taking a non-compromising approach to standards.

Who was the best boss you ever had and why?

I'm going to be controversial and say that person doesn't exist.

In any boss that I've had, I've always recognised, that just as in every human being, every boss has got strengths and has got weaknesses or things that we just must live with.

For me, the opportunity was to learn from everybody, the good and the bad. Even the bosses I didn't enjoy working with, they had towering strengths, and they had flaws. I think that, for me, is what the human condition is about. Rather than, this person being the best, or this person being the worst, I found the good in everybody, and I found those characteristics and traits that I didn't want to replicate.

For me, personally, there is something built in me that I don't have a favourite anything.

What's your favourite restaurant? I can't answer the question.

I could probably say what's the preferred Indian restaurant, or preferred Italian, but even then, I would be compromising, right?

Because if it's a posh Indian I'd like to go here, if its as cheap as chips, I like to go here. I don't subscribe to this notion of the best. What does it mean?

Is just a concept that I struggle with. It's the same with the worst. What's the worst restaurant I've even been to? It is difficult. I can tell you what the restaurant is that I've had bad service in, or I've had really bad food here, or the quality is not very good here. That concept of best and worst I struggle with, just as a human being. It's been too prescribed, I think.

What was the greatest challenge you faced as a middle manager?

There are so many challenges. I think the thing I learned after the event, is that there is this disease in middle management. Which is the disease of making assumptions about the people that are very senior to you, what they would like and not like.

Middle management is the toughest job, because you are at that point in your career where you can't really complain upwards, and you have got to absorb all the complaints that come from below you.

You're at that level say in the retail business, you're an area manager or a regional manager and the store managers are bitching and moaning about stuff that comes down the pipe, right?

You have no choice. You've got to implement what's been decided. You have to absorb that complaint of "oh it will never work; oh, I don't want to do it. We can't cut costs; we can't do it."

You've got to absorb that.

You can't pass it up the line. If there are things that aren't working, you can pass it up the line, but the emotion that comes from below, is difficult to pass on.

What you have, is rational instruction being passed down, you have emotional response coming up, and you're the guy, the one person that sits in the middle and must absorb that.

You must filter from both sides.

You must do that filtering, if you're a team exec like me, you filter what goes to the board, what goes to colleagues, and you do it easily because you've had many years of experience. As a middle manager though, that's one of the toughest positions throughout your career.

There's this thing, I don't think it's necessarily a problem for middle managers to solve, I think it's for senior managers in the organisation.

If I stick with an area manager example, one of the things you'll hear middle managers say if a store manager comes up with a bright idea is "I could never take that to the board."

My question is, 'Is that true?' One of the problems that you have when you get to board level is what's being filtered out. What aren't you hearing? What truths aren't you getting to? If you're not getting to the truth, you're not spending enough time at grass roots level, and, you've got a filter. The filter is deciding for you what's good and what's not. It's not always easy to understand the impacts at that time.

You should take it upon yourself to try and find out what information is relevant and pass on the right information.

I think another challenge when you get to middle management, is to start tailoring the approach you have. If you're a retail store manager, effectively, you run it in a certain way as staff come and go, and they must fit into your way of running the store. When you're an area manager, you now have, let's say, 12 store managers, each one wanting to run it their own way.

Now, suddenly, you're interacting with senior management, you're interacting with those above you. You might be interacting with suppliers or other people. Now, you must start managing people according to the situation. Of course, you aren't used to that. You're used to doing one size fits all.

How do you decide how to get the best from people? How do you decide on how to vary your style to get the best out of a new direct report? I think that kind of situational leadership is quite important.

When you first get your first rung of middle management. You are typically managing people who have done what you do.

Or you've done their job, or it might be supervisory in nature and there are many people doing the same job and if you're an area manager you are managing a group of store managers, all who do the same job. The difficulty comes further up, when you are still in the middle management ranks, and you must start managing people who do different jobs or do different jobs to the one you've ever done. That's point at which you must start managing experts who know more than you.

That's the first time you must start managing people who do a job that you've never done.

Another challenge is how do you assess talent? If you're a middle manager, you're managing a group of managers. How do you assess potential, and how do you assess talent? First, do you know that there's a difference between performance and potential?

What is the difference? Because there is a big difference to me, the 'potential' piece is crucial. Performance is rather straight forward, because you normally have a set of KPIs, or you can compare behaviours, stuff like that. In terms of potential, for me there are three types of potential that you must look for.

There's the potential to expand within your role. If I am just somebody who is doing a bunch of work, and you can give me more work, you can give me more responsibility within what I do. That's a form of potential, so expansion within role. I've got the potential to become a subject matter expert, to become an absolute expert in what I do.

If you're in marketing or HR you might become a pricing specialist, or you might become a learning and development specialist. This is the potential for mastery, if you'd like. To be a subject matter expert. The other potential is the potential for promotion, in effect to move up to the next level of management.

Those are three different things.

One of the things when you're managing young people with maybe different ambition levels, with different desires, with different ability, is where do you spend your time?

How are you coaching, training, and developing those people? Typically what I did and what I see is other people trying to do is coach everybody.

Without standing back and asking 'What is the potential here?' And 'How am I coaching them?' I think the last thing, and the single most important thing for any leader at any level to have is self-awareness.

It's the single biggest skill that you can have. When I talk about self-awareness, I talk about the ability to know what you're good at, know what you're bad at, what you prefer doing, and what you don't like doing. It's about ability and preference. It's the ability to tell the truth to yourself.

What you tell your boss I don't care. What you tell yourself is really, important.

That's what governs and drives your behaviour.

The ability to tell yourself the truth, because that will be the thing that enables your self-development. That will be the thing that is a catalyst for change if there is an area that you really want to make progress and improvement on.

What was the biggest mistake you made when you were a middle manager?

I have very few regrets in life, but I once had a boss who I made life very difficult for.

I was good at what I did. I was in the right job kind of adding significant value, and I didn't want to report to this individual.

It's because I perceived that they couldn't help me. I perceived that they weren't the right person for me, not somebody I wanted to respect or learn from. They used to ask me a lot of questions. That used to frustrate me. I would misbehave in answering the questions. What I discovered a bit later is, the reason they were asking me a lot of questions, was they were genuinely curious or fascinated by why I made certain decisions, and the success I got.

They were wanting to learn from me. Equally, if they had spotted a few things they where worried about, they were better than me and I could learn from them. This boss tried to take an approach of learning from me and allowing me to learn from him, but I had made my mind up out of the gate that this wasn't the right person. My behaviour was less than exemplary, and there's very few things I look back on and say I regret, but that's one. I think, actually my behaviour and the way I treated them was shocking . The way I approached it. I look back on that and think that wasn't great, and I've learned from it.

I think that's probably one of the catalysts of me looking for the good and the bad in anybody. That catalyst for you can learn from everyone.

What personal qualities do you see in the best middle managers?

A couple of things, I haven't talked about. The **self-awareness** piece is very important. **Flexibility of style** and being able to flex your style to help others. Then, I think this notion of **personal accountability**. Taking responsibility for what is effectively your sphere of influence, regardless of what happens. When mistakes are made by your team, when mistakes get made by others. It's about taking personal accountability.

This notion that you should always look in the mirror first before you look at others. Even if a mistake has happened, or there is a situation created, even if it is not quite of your making, you should always look in the mirror and ask yourself what have I done to contribute to this? Before bollocking the other person, take that personal accountability. I think that is really important.

The other thing is never underestimate the **power of recognition**.

When people aren't successful, and don't do a good job, 90% of the time it is a failure of leadership, not a failure of the individual. Not every time, but often. Then when people are on the right track, when people are on the right course, it's recognising that, and reinforcing that behaviour.

I don't understand this notion of 'Why should I say thank you, or why should I reward you because that's what they are paid to do. That's in the job description. Why thank an accounts payable person for processing 250 invoices a day?' Well, because it took great effort and great skill on the part of that person to do their job and you should recognise them for that. I think it goes a long way. It gets you much more engagement than pay.

What skills do you think middle managers should focus on developing to ensure their effectiveness over their career?

I think as you climb the ladder you must identify the learning curve you have.

What's the technical learning curve that I need to come up, and what's the leadership behaviour and experience curve that I need to come up? Those two things are different.

If I take a new job, what are the technical things that are different? It's a different product. It's a different service. It's a different way of working. It's a different culture, whatever. Those things are all things that you can go and learn, and typically things that you would expect to be on your induction plan. When I joined Starbucks, I went to work in a store. I went to Seattle and did three months training. I worked in a store for four weeks. At a managing director level, I learned how to be a barista. I learned how to be a store manager. I learned how to be an area manager. I learned how to be a regional manager.

I did it accelerated at three months. That's technically something that you can learn. What they don't teach you, is the cultural stuff. They don't teach you what's the leadership thing. One of the things, and this is a senior management example, not middle management, I was expected to do was to do a lot of public affairs and government affairs. Some of that was technical, but some of that was behavioural. How do you show up representing an enterprise, not just representing what you do? It's mostly finding out what are the technical things, and what are the leadership things that you need to be successful.

Making sure that you spend, probably more time on the leadership stuff. Of course, you need to learn the technical stuff, but it's leadership behaviours that will make you successful. That's what you need to know and that is what you need to do.

What do you know now that you wish you knew as a middle manager?

I think the self-awareness piece is a big one for me. That is important. The other thing is that when you are in a leadership position, you should only do those tasks that only you can do.

As a chief exec, I should only do those tasks that only the chief exec can do. If you're a regional manager of a retail business, you should only do those tasks that only a regional manager can do or should do. If not, then you are either doing somebody else's job for them, or you're working on something that isn't core to the mission.

What's your one Tip for the Top?

One tip for the top, I would say is never be intimidated. You should never be intimidated by people who are better or smarter than you, ever. Hire for diversity, do not hire in your image.

Diversity of thinking, diversity of thought, diversity of style.

Plus, all of the other physical diversity attributes that we talk about.

Diversity of thought and style I think are really, important.

I suppose there is a bit in there for also middle management which is don't hold somebody else back because of your own anxieties and insecurities or your own career aspirations, because it will eventually backfire.

You should be able to achieve the abilities of your potential and your desire, if you like, and nobody else coming through should necessarily get in the way of that. If somebody else comes through that has potential to be your boss in the future, if you're hiring the next chief exec, that's got to be a good thing. So what if one day you'll end up working for somebody that you hired. If they're the right person to do that right job at that time.

It is bringing us back to the self-awareness point.

I know what I'm good at. I know what I'm not. I know what I like to do, and I know what I don't. That probably won't allow you to get in the way.

One other thing I would say is subscribe to the hierarchy. The hierarchy always needs to be company first, function second, self-third.

You always need to put the mission of the enterprise ahead of your own personal mission. Or that of your function.

What is the one book you'd recommend to every middle manager?

Servant Leadership by Robert Greenleaf

What two things have struck you most from what was said?

What one thing will you do differently/employ as a result of what you've learnt from this chapter?

4

David James

Co-founder, Looop, a learning technology business.

David is regular conference speaker and host of the Learning & Development podcast. He had a successful corporate career working in senior learning and development roles for the likes of NatWest, Lehman Brothers and Disney. He has worked in Europe and Africa.

What was your best memory or achievement when you were a middle manager?

I'd say it was a memory more than an achievement. It was being party to key conversations at Disney. So whether it be in business leadership meetings in which I often played a part, whether that was to consider the talent or the people development element to it or whether I was just in a very senior business meeting, waiting for my turn to present.

I was in meetings, very confidential meetings at the time about Disney's plans to launch a streaming service. And the meeting, it's was huge, exciting. Another meeting was when one of the Pirates of the Caribbean movies was being launched and the conversation around the room went something like this, "We only find out what movies are going to be shown in any week on a particular day." To which someone else replied, "Well, that's bonkers. Have we thought about buying back all the cinemas?"

It's then I realised I was in some seriously heavy-hitting meetings. When an organisation has so much clout, has so much vision and you've got such smart people in the room. I'd say that my greatest memory was being privy to those meetings, and leads onto everything I'm pretty much going to be talking about. I was able to see how very senior people operate, get the right things done and bring people with them. I'd say that that sowed the seeds for my success in my role at Disney. But the greatest memory was you really do see what's going on behind the scenes.

Who was the best boss you've ever had, and why?

I think there were three key bosses in my career, and I'd say that none of them were perfect and they were good for me in different ways. The first one I'd say was my first training manager, a guy called Robin Fenner.

This must've been my third job. I was a junior barrister's clerk and it was just work, just get stuff done. And then I worked at the Woolwich Building Society, and management was inconsistent, at best. And then I met Robin who was faciliative in his approach and wanted to know what I thought.

I was really caught by surprise by the conversations we would have. Now, I'd say that Robin had the biggest impact on my style because I'd rather not steam in with authority and just expect the best of people. I'd prefer to give them enough opportunity to develop themselves. So, I'd say that he's had the biggest impact on my style, but my two bosses at Disney, one of them was really invested in my progression. I got promoted three times in six years at Disney, which is unheard of there.

My then boss, the one who I took over from said; "We need to take a look at the promotion criteria."

I remember thinking that he could have said that when I was out of the room! There was the boss who had an enormous amount invested in my progression, but the problem was she was a bit of a micro-manager.

Another gave me an enormous amount of freedom, which felt like an enormous amount of rope to hang myself with at times, but at other times it was an incredible amount of autonomy. So, I'd say those three.

What was the greatest challenge you faced when you were a middle manager?

It wasn't one individual part; it was a huge aspect of the job. At Disney, when you were in one of the countries, whether that be the UK, France, Germany, Spain, you were accountable to local stakeholders and you did what you knew was right to get stuff done. At a global level they sought standardisation and the buying of systems, the development of programs. Middle management, you tried to find a way to get the standardised stuff to link to local needs when you had local people who were close to the business. So, you're trying to drive consistency and standardisation as well as progression to a load of people who kind of knew what they needed to do.

So, it was kind of like being stuck in the middle. You're the jam in the sandwich. It was one of the reasons I left because I felt that I was getting in the way. I'd gone from a position of really knowing my market, really knowing my stakeholders. I got promoted because I was doing all the right stuff and holding together, which is 14 disparate organisations that came under one roof and really making a difference.

Then you go up to that middle level, at which you're the jam rather than the bread and then there was a lot of schmoozing. There were a lot of meetings. I didn't feel as if I was achieving much at all. The remit of the role was to try to inch everything forward a little bit at a time, keep everybody on board, hold some people at bay, have a say to try to influence. But there was so little opportunity to influence the global element and you just feel pretty pointless at times.

There were a lot of professional schmoozers at Disney at the time. But I just didn't fancy it. That's when I had a reaction and realised that I want to know that the stuff I do on a day-to-day basis is all about getting the right stuff done. And that's why I decided to come out and work in a start-up where it was the antithesis of inching stuff forward or sometimes, sideways. So, driving it forward. That was the biggest challenge.

I know that because my successor told me that he was having the same conversations two years on. I knew then I'd made the right decision because I couldn't see myself doing it for another minute, let alone for another couple of years.

What was the biggest mistake you made when you were a middle manager?

I'd say the biggest mistake, if I valued this more, was not sticking around long enough. I left Disney after two years, as I mentioned before, because I was frustrated, but now I know that it was part of the development and I needed to earn more currency. I've learnt so much since then. I think there's a Harvard report on it that says that at director level and above, it could take up to three years to get your groove on, to really feel as if you're really performing. And I think that every now and again and wonder what would've happened if I'd just sucked it up for a little bit longer. Now, that said, I'm much more fulfilled in my work here and I don't think I made any mistakes that were worthy of note.

I fall out with people, but I don't think that was a mistake. You think someone's a dick and we're going to clash. And so, I don't see that as a mistake, but for the first couple of years after I left, I thought if I'd have had a career break and then gone back, I would've had a bit more perspective. But two years is nothing in a transition into that level. I think I was a bit hard on myself. I could have been more patient and maybe recognise the little inches forward as wins. And I didn't. I didn't take any pleasure in inching forward at all.

I do see friends who are still there who have gone above the level I was, who had the patience and who are now flourishing at much more senior level.

And, as I said, I don't regret it because eight years at Disney was plenty of time for me. I do now see that there was a way to get through and maybe there would've been more growth for me.

What personal qualities do you see in the best middle managers?

It sounds like a cliché, but I think the first one is **vision**. And I think that it is the ability to share with your team and your stakeholders, your clients, your customers, how the world will be better if they follow you.

So, vision, I think, is absolutely critical at the right time. With a dysfunctional team, I joined as director there wasn't time for vision. That was around tactics. But I think that the best middle managers I've seen have been able to share their vision, which doesn't have to be grand, but there just needs to be something for people to grab hold of.

There's also got to be **clarity and principles**. I believe people want to know who you are really and what's important to you. I also think style is incredibly important and I think brand sits within that, as well.

Again, I know this sounds so cliché, but what I mean by brand is the ability to profile yourself right, in order to influence people and get the resources you need to represent your team.

When you leave your team to go to a senior meeting, you are representing them. I think we've all worked for people who've said, "I'm off to so-and-so meeting," and you think, "Oh, God, you're embarrassing us all."

So, I do think that there's an element of your own **personal brand** which is used in order to profile you but yourself and your team. And then the last one is **influence**. I can't say enough for middle management, if you can't influence people, you have nothing, you're dead in the water.

I think this is such an important element. I've seen so many middle managers fail because they may have had great ideas and they may have had their own technical professional know-how, but they didn't understand the culture of the business and they couldn't get the right stuff done.

What skills as opposed to qualities do you think middle managers should focus on developing to ensure their effectiveness over their career?

Organisational savvy. Their ability to recognise what is going on within an organisation, the expected and rewarded norms and behaviours, and then be able to navigate that without being a political animal. And to both protect and profile their team members and help them to develop at the same time. I think organisational savvy, the ability to be savvy within an organisation requires so much. It requires the brand, it requires the influence, but it can also protect you from finding yourself excluded from any groups that have an important stake in both your ability to deliver results and grow in your career.

What do you now know that you wish you knew when you were a middle manager?

To cut myself some slack. Nobody's looking at me thinking, "He's failing because he's not delivering." The schmoozing and the moving stuff forward were enough.

Things change quicker around you than you think they are. As an example, I left Disney for a couple of reasons. One was that I fell out with someone who had an important stake in my career. Now, I didn't leave because they were pushing me out. But they left the business a year later and so if I'd stayed it would have been a huge relief and I would have progressed.

I think that when you are outside of an organisation looking back in, time goes at a normal pace or faster. Yet when you're in it, it feels like nothing's going to change.

So, my advice is don't be so hard yourself. Ride challenges as if they are waves, so swim on top or on a surfboard, that way you can seek some perspective.

I think I took it like a scuba diver. And then you just get lost and all you see is murk.

What's your one tip for the top?

Bring people with you.

You must. And that means absolutely everybody. You can't prioritise one group over another. But you can and should prioritise who and when. I think that Jose Mourinho, was great at the us-and-them part, at Porto and Chelsea. "Everybody hates us, or everybody underestimates us, but we'll show them." And it worked at Inter.

Then he went to Real Madrid and then he tried a different thing which was, to create animosity within the group. He tried to show certain players that they weren't 'the man here'.

And suddenly, he's creating friction within his group rather than keeping them together. He did the same when he returned to Chelsea and at Man United and it showed. It cost him his job. You've got to bring everybody with you. You don't divide and conquer ever, and you don't neglect a group.

Now, it's not about being everyone's friend and it's not about not being inauthentic. It is being savvy of truly understanding that you can operate with your eyes wide open and you can bring people with you and you can challenge people, but don't be a dick and they will respect you. If you don't bring people with you, then you will find that your ability to influence will be limited as well as your career.

What's one book you'd recommend every middle manager read?

Survival of the Savvy, by Rick Brandon.

It's one of those books. It turns the light on for you. So as you read it, it turns the light on and you can't un-see what you've seen. You'll look at your organisation, you'll think of people that you work with. I went on a program that was designed around that book. I was with a load of peers and somebody, who was head of a department, said, "I don't want to play the game." And the trainer said, "You've got no choice. You are in the game." So, if you won't play the game you will be played.

What is really going on is that people are going about their business with good intentions, with bad intentions, indifferent intentions, and the world is not black or white.

There's a hell of a lot of grey and dynamics change a lot, as well. Some colleagues might be under pressure, some might be feeling an incorrect sense of superiority. You've got to be able to see all of this. There'll be some people covering their backside because they're lazy or they've got a bad reputation and now they're trying to sling mud in another's direction. You have to be able to see this and you have to able to develop a network and your currency in order to get the right stuff done.

If you don't invest in your organisational savvy, you are letting yourself down and you're not going to be able to achieve your aims within an organisation. Now, I hear about organisations that aren't political, and good luck to them. I've never worked in an organisation where it's not political.

Understanding what the dynamics are, your role within that and what you could do in order to better operate, I think is absolutely essential. And the longer you leave it, you are giving time away instead of building the currency. Currency is so important. It is what you are trading at any time in order to help you get the right stuff done. So that's my big thing.

What's one question I haven't asked you that you think I should have and what would be the answer then?

How does one transition from management to C-suite?

At the C-suite level there is loads more autonomy. It looks like loads more autonomy because no one's giving you work. But it's only by the closeness to your stakeholders and your mining and interpretation of information that allows you to know that you are making the right decisions and the right bets. No one's asking you about your work until maybe it's too late. If anyone's asking about your work, it's too late.

You're lunching and having coffee with senior folks and maybe there's not a lot of work being talked about. But, again, that's important. You're mining, you're profiling. It's so different from management, really. As a manager, I'd say that there's still a great deal of emphasis on doing, but as a C-suite executive, if you're still doing, you're doing the job wrong. You're missing the mark. So, I'd say that there is an enormous difference and it is more in the way that people treat you and what's expected of you, and it's not explicitly said. That's the big difference. That's what I think.

My advice here is to invest in your peer group. I think that Patrick Lencioni calls it your "Team number one." It is the people who are reporting to your boss at any level. There is work on your profile. Develop your savvy, beware of kissing up and kicking down. I think it's absolutely critical.

Perception is as powerful as results, but don't sacrifice one for the other. Know and own your currency. You've got to know what people value within you and what you've got to trade. There's so much. Currency is knowing the right people and allowing them to stand next to you.

Or, information is currency, as well. Don't ignore signals and at that level I'd say it's more signals than explicit stuff. If you're not being invited to the lunches, that's a signal. If information isn't coming to you first hand, that's a signal. I think the last one is appreciate the fact that you may not feel comfortable maybe for years.

What two things have struck you most from what was said?

What one thing will you do differently/employ as a result of what you've learnt from this chapter?

5

Doug Strycharczyk

CEO, AQR International

Doug founded AQR in 1989 and now works in 80 countries. AQR is recognised as a thought leader in people and organisational development particularly around its pioneering work on Mental Toughness.

Doug worked as a middle and senior manager in Goodyear, Wedgwood, Decca and briefly in West Midlands Passenger Transport Executive and finally as Head of Operations and Head of HR for Castrol UK.

A recognised author, his books have been translated in several languages.

What was the greatest challenge you faced as a middle manager?

All of my roles were to do with managing change. The most consistent challenge was to bring others with you when many felt threatened – staff and other managers.

What was the biggest mistake you made when you were a middle manager?

Assuming that everyone could see the logic of an argument and would accept it as such. People aren't rational although much management theory is based on that notion. You could often be stopped in your tracks and have to work out why.

What personal qualities do you see in the best middle managers?

Having a **goal** and delivering results.

Understanding what it means for others to work with you to achieve those goals – and attending to their needs as well as your own.

Understanding **team working**. I mean really understanding team working. Not just "my team is OK it's everyone else ..." but engaging with everyone in the organisation.

Being a role model – practice what you preach.

What I am really describing is leadership.

What skills do you think middle managers should focus on developing to ensure their effectiveness over their career?

There are two sets:

Leadership. Not only developing effectiveness in the way described below but also understanding the importance of leadership style and its relationship with the situation. This means that throughout your career you should reflect on your leadership style, check that it is appropriate for your setting and be prepared to adjust it.

People and organisations grow and develop, managers must grow with them too.

The other area is not so much a skill as a key enabler. Its Mental Toughness. It is fundamentally important in acquiring and developing skills. It's where openness to learning sits and about having confidence in your abilities.

It's like putting the fundamentals down to enable you to build your career on solid foundations.

What do you know now that you wish you knew as a middle manager?

The need to connect with people – staff, clients and suppliers – as individuals.

What's your one Tip for the Top?

Develop your mental toughness. Without it, it can be a rough journey, you will feel every knock on the way and you might never get there. The research shows that the more senior you are the more mentally tough the individual.

What is the one book you'd recommend to any and every middle manager?

I don't think there is any one book in the same way there isn't one way to be a great leader or manager. I see too many who become mesmerised with a set of ideas they once learned. The trick is to read and read and critically examine everything you come across – particularly checking for two things: is it based on sound theory and does it really work?

In this era there are lots of good sources of information and ideas through the internet.

In hindsight, I probably learned more form my managers than I ever did from books although books helped to give a structure and perspective with which I could balance what I experienced.

Who was the best boss you ever had and why?

This is tricky. I was fortunate to work for many good bosses. Probably the best, the one who learned most from was someone I worked closely with rather than him being my boss.

His name was Les Challacombe. He ran Coalport China – a very successful high-end business employing some 1100 people. I have never worked with anyone who inspired so many people to achieve so much. Everyone was loyal, committed to what he was seeking to achieve and engaged. Although it seemed random, he would spend at least 30% of every day walking the operation speaking with people ensuring that he was seen at least weekly by everyone.

He wasn't a boss who sat behind a desk in his office. He was quite different from bosses I had grown used to. When I asked him about it he simply responded: "Why should they be interested in me and what I am trying to do if I don't show an interest in them and their issues?"

What question haven't I asked that you think I should have?

There may be a number – all about the future and what it holds for management and leadership. Three issues keep bubbling to the surface. The first is professionalism, adopting soundly based practice and avoiding faddism. The second is agility, the ability to deal with the VUCA (volatile, uncertain, complex, ambiguous) world and thirdly, evidence based practice, checking what you do works and if it doesn't learning from that.

What two things have struck you most from what was said?

What one thing will you do differently/employ as a result of what you've learnt from this chapter?

6

Dr Diane Wright

Head of International, Faculty of Business & Law, Manchester Metropolitan University

Dr Diane Wright has had a varied and full career. She started out in marketing in the male-dominated car care industry for brands like Turtle Wax, Red X. Colour Magic etc, before moving into 'new media' as the marketing director for an agency.

She then moved over into higher education, lecturing before becoming head of department, and then ultimately, the head of international for the faculty of business and law. She also ran her own retail business for five years.

What was your best memory or achievement as a middle manager?

It depends actually what you think of achievement and whether you talk about achievement for the business or achievement for yourself, in your career.

In terms of the business, as a sales marketing manager for a car care chemicals company. It was a very difficult time in car care chemicals because cars were becoming much more solid and reliable, they didn't rust as much, exhausts didn't drop off as much and things like that. Probably the main achievement, was keeping a very, very stable business going and not losing business to the competition. Introducing new products, at a time when the market was changing so much. So, I think being able to maintain a good market share was quite important, even though the market was declining.

It was a really, enjoyable time. We were all quite young, and so there were always places where you could make your career. I loved working there and had some good friends. But it was tough, and I learned so much, I really did. I think really being able to keep your eyes open and ears open for opportunities, throwing yourself headlong into doing stuff is important.

Sometimes I hear people saying, "well that's not my job, I'm not doing that." But I think really being willing to get your hands dirty and get stuck in and find out about the business is so important.

On reflection another big achievement in this particular point in time was survival, because I hadn't been there that long when all the brand managers and all the marketing managers were made redundant. There were six of us that were assistant brand managers and we had to step up.

It was terrifying because we were assistant brand managers, and we hadn't got that experience that the others had. But that gave me such a massive, massive opportunity to learn so much. I think if you can learn something new every day, and keep your interest going, that's so important.

Who was the best boss you ever had and why?

I've been fortunate to have a lot of good bosses, and I put down my progression partially to these great bosses I've had.

I had three male bosses that were great, and I've had two female bosses that were great. And to be honest, I wouldn't like to say who'd been the best. It's easy to say one was the best if you happen to have progressed far with that particular boss.

At the university, Dennis, who was my boss at the time, I think I probably progressed quickest with him. And so, it would be easy for me to say, yeah actually he's my best because I went from being a senior lecturer up to an associate dean. He recognised in me something that was a bit like him.

But one guy at Holtz who I had was a great boss and he promoted me. I mean you always like your bosses who promote you, don't you? I think he was quite brave in doing that, because they expected some of the men to be promoted. Which is what happened with Dennis, there were two older guys who were senior to me and he didn't promote them, just me.

And then I've had more recent bosses, one woman who was great because she made me quite aspirational, and she'd lead by example, and people just warmed to her.

And then my final boss, she was a great boss because she kind of let me get on with things and trusted me. That appeals to me, not somebody on your back all the time, but if you need help, they'd be there to go to.

What was the greatest challenge you faced as a middle manager?

I think it was working in a very masculine environment, that was very challenging. When I said that the six assistant brand managers stayed but everybody else was made redundant, I found out through the back door really, that the other five who were guys had been made junior brand managers and I hadn't. There was absolutely no reason why not, I had no idea why that was the case, other than I was the most recent recruit. But not by two years or anything like that, by a few months.

I went to the straight sales and marketing director, and I asked him to explain why this had happened. He said, "Oh I didn't think you'd be interested". He just never thought that I would have that career aspiration. He then promoted me

He also said to me once, "Don't leave it too late, start thinking about having a family." I replied: "I'm not even married yet!" It was the cultural stigma and discrimination of the time.

What was the biggest mistake you made when you were a middle manager?

Well I think it's the converse of what I've just said. I think my mistake was allowing things to happen a bit too much, and not recognising the issues that you face as being female. So, I think that was a mistake, I could have been a little bit more assertive about that looking back.

I think another mistake, was doing something I didn't enjoy for a couple of years. I worked, for a new media agency called Moon Fish, and I just hated it. I really hated it, and I stuck it out and stuck it out.

Now that could be a good thing because I learnt lots, but maybe I stuck it out for too long and sometimes I think, I have the tendency to think, "I can't give up on this." I didn't realise that I needed to be proactive in another direction and look for something else, and I stuck it out for too long.

When I was marketing manager at Holtz, we had a boss who believed in management by conflict. So, it was a difficult time, and I'd have people who would moan to me and want to leave. I'd say, "It's in your hands this, it's all in your hands, you know you control your destiny. So, if you've decided that this isn't right for you, well start looking for something else, you take control of it."

I think point is important. We must take control of what we do and don't just accept that something isn't working for us, but we must take control. Because nobody else will do it for us.

Resilience is a hugely important. So, on the one hand don't keep doing something that really isn't good for you or for career or even your health, but there is something in being resilient. Not taking things personally, saying: "I know I've done that wrong but let's keep going, let me try again, let me learn from that." So for me developing resilience is an important factor as well.

What personal qualities do you see in the best middle managers?

The ability to **get things done through other people**. And if you can, command respect, you're more likely to get people doing things and doing what you need.

Being a good **communicator** is also essential. Because people sometimes misunderstand what you're saying, and they interpret that in different ways. So being able to communicate clearly to people so they understand what you want from them, I think is important as well.

So, **communication**, **commanding respect** and **resilience**, are essential qualities if you want to progress. Especially, as in middle management, you're in quite a difficult position, really. Because you're sandwiched between senior management and your team, and you're a bit like an egg timer in the middle. Where everything's coming down to you from the top and you've got it coming up from the bottom.

It's a matter of keeping a handle on what's happening, managing upwards, and managing downwards as well. And I think that is a very difficult position to be in sometimes.

What skills do you think middle managers should focus on developing to ensure their effectiveness over their career?

Well I suppose those skills that I've mentioned, it's not about technical ability. For example I was speaking to the general manager of AO.com, and he said, "If we want to recruit forklift truck drivers, we don't recruit people who can drive a forklift truck. We recruit people who have got the personality traits that fit in our culture."

Sometimes you can see that somebody can do a job, but actually what you want is for them to not just do the job, but be committed and play a bigger role in an organisation.

I also think it is about managing upwards and downwards and about building relationships as well.

What do you know now that you wish you knew as a middle manager?

I don't think I had enough confidence as middle manager. I think I was more capable than I thought I was. That might be the gender thing, I don't know. I certainly wasn't as forceful as I should have been.

I touched on this before, I let things happen a little more than I should have done. I should have taken a little bit control of things and been confident in what I believed in or my gut feel or however you want to say it. I think I should have been more assertive. And I probably wasn't. I think people need to have more confidence in their abilities. Some of that might be because until you are a little more mature you don't build up the resilience quite so much. And so, you don't want to feel bad about something, you don't want to feel that you've not done a good job. So sometimes you might try something or not try something because you're worried about not doing well at it. I think you have to bite the bullet sometimes and go for it.

So, in summary, have a go and be confident in your own abilities.

What's your one Tip for the Top?

It would be really what I've said, to be honest. Don't be frightened to just have a go at something and take that step. The people who I feel are successful are the ones who have thought, "yeah, I can do that. I'll go for that". They've got a bit of grit about them, and don't worry about the knocks, you can take the knocks.

What is the one book you'd recommend to every middle manager?

The author (rather than a single book) that had meant the most to me was a sociologist whose works I used as the basis for my PhD, Pierre Bourdieu. I didn't agree with everything he said but looking at his works helped me to see my career and life as a whole.

Bourdieu claims that everyone possesses different amounts of 'capital' which could be social capital (networks), economic capital (finances) and cultural capital (taste). He also believes that the capital we possess determines our place in society and in what he calls 'fields' – and the world of business could be such a field. He believes that our places are fairly 'fixed' in these fields and we can't do much to change our position.

This is what I found interesting and I disagreed as I believe that we can change the amount and type of capital we have and our 'place' in the world. So, we could increase our social capital by developing our networks We could also include 'academic capital' as a form of capital which gives us a certain amount of power in certain fields. I was also interested in how men and women have different types of capital which prevents women from competing in certain fields.

What question haven't I asked that you think I should have?

Well, it could be something about how as a senior manager that you would do things differently, or how they would want middle managers to behave.

Because, as I became more senior in an organisation, I realised that when I was a middle manager I would try and get on with stuff myself and wouldn't always go to the senior manager and say: "Look, I'm having a bit of a problem with this and how would you suggest I do this?"

As a senior manager I would rather know when my team was struggling with something and they come to me. I think it's important for middle managers to understand that senior managers want to know where you're up to with things and are open to you asking for advice.

What two things have struck you most from what was said?

What one thing will you do differently/employ as a result of what you've learnt from this chapter?

7

Gary Kibble

Marketing Director, Sainsburys Argos

Gary joined WH Smiths as a Marketing Graduate Trainee after graduating in Business Studies. After a few years learning the 'art' of marketing, Gary moved into buying and joined the Board at the age of 28 as Commercial Director, Books.

After 10 successful years at WH Smith, Gary was asked to join the Barclay Brother owned business, Shop Direct. Shortly after joining the owners also purchased the Littlewoods business and the work began to take two fiercely competitive brands and create one. The business transformation was critical to underpin the growth ambitions of the newly formed group. The traditional catalogue retailer embarked on a significant transformation programme that shifted the business from catalogue retailing to be a world class digital leader. After 10 amazing years at Shop Direct, Gary joined Mothercare as Chief Customer Officer with a Global remit before snapping up an opportunity to join Sainsburys Argos.

What was your best memory or achievement as a middle manager?

My best achievement was probably launching The Full Monty or Titanic on DVD at W H Smiths. We created an impressive campaign that engaged store managers and excited customers. The outcome was significant market share growth and a fundamental improvement in the commercial performance of the function. My best memory was probably attending the worldwide premiere of Godzilla in Madison Square Gardens...flying in a seaplane around the Statue of Liberty. A once in a lifetime opportunity.

Who was the best boss you ever had and why?

Without doubt it was Mark Newton-Jones who I worked for at Shop Direct and whom I 'followed' to Mothercare. He shaped my most informative years in business. He had a fairly unique skill of setting clear direction, 'lighting the fire' and empowering those around him to make stuff happen.

What was the greatest challenge you faced as a middle manager?

It must be the balance of knowing when to 'do' and when to lead. To some extent being a middle-manager is the hardest position to adopt. You are still hungry for the next big thing, you try and balance leading and empowering others whilst having a natural temptation to 'get on and do'

What was the biggest mistake you made when you were a middle manager?

No knowing when I was a leader and when I was a friend

What personal qualities do you see in the best middle managers?

High degrees of **integrity** and **trust** with a thorough understanding of how to get the job done, all topped with the ability to **lead, motivate** and **inspire**. Easy right?!

What skills do you think middle managers should focus on developing to ensure their effectiveness over their career?

Communication, task focus with a growing passion to lead and develop others.

What do you know now that you wish you knew as a middle manager?

That it would all happen 'in good time' – don't rush, don't waste the best years of your working life away wondering when it will happen!

What's your one Tip for the Top?

To always be the best possible version of you, work hard make your intentions clear and back yourself.

What is the one book you'd recommend to every middle manager?

Either the Chimp Paradox or, as a lighter read and a good balance between a business book and a brilliant autobiography, Clive Woodward's 'Winning'.

What two things have struck you most from what was said?

What one thing will you do differently/employ as a result of what you've learnt from this chapter?

8

Graham Wilson

The UK's #1 Leadership Coach

Founder of the Success Factory and author of several leadership books including Leadership Laid Bare.

What was your best memory or achievement as a middle manager?

Seeing a vision come to light has to be one of the best feelings, yet my biggest thrill was always seeing my team develop and individuals move on to greater things. Seeing people grow with confidence and achieve things they thought impossible was always the greatest buzz for me.

Who was the best boss you ever had and why?

Daddy Kumbu was a giant of a man, he 'guided' me through basic training in the Army, he taught me on my drill course, and he inspired me to be the best I could be. He was also an ex-international rugby player for Fiji, who could have played in any position around the park due to his skill and passion for the sport.

He was also the most caring leader I've met. Don't get me wrong, he wasn't soft, far from it! He was also one of the toughest and hardest men I've ever met. The sort of person you would want to have on your side when you go to war!

I've met many great leaders during my career in the military and one of the biggest differences I noticed when leaving the military and working in the commercial world was the lack of pride, care and compassion of many leaders in the commercial world.

I like the quote stating that, "leadership isn't about being in charge of people, it's about caring for the people in your charge." I can remember many 'grilling's' from Daddy Kumbu, which were all done from a place of care and compassion. He wanted us to be successful and be able to operate in tough environments. His teachings were hard at the time but all done with the right intent.

I can also remember playing rugby with him for the first time. We were playing another Corps and he was our team manager. He was at the pitch way before anyone else, making sure the dressing room was clean and set up correctly. All the shirts on the right pegs with shorts and socks all lined up. That was over 36 years ago and I can still remember how it made me feel when I walked into the dressing room. I felt full of pride and confidence. Just to put this in context, this was a Regimental Sergeant Major (The Boss) and ex-international player cleaning the dressing room and hanging up the kit!

What was the greatest challenge you faced as a middle manager?

I can always remember one of the first meetings I had as I moved into the corporate world from the Army. The advice I was given was that I had to realise there were people in the organisation wanting my projects to fail. I didn't believe him until the next governance meeting and a Senior Leader was killing one of my projects.

The greatest challenge I had was always around the politics and egos. Managing upwards was a key skill I had to develop really quickly. Otherwise you end up with Senior Leaders meddling with your work. You have to manage the stakeholder anxiety gap and learn how to use invisible leadership.

What was the biggest mistake you made when you were a middle manager?

I can think of many mistakes or learning opportunities! The biggest was thinking that I always had to have the answers. Often, I didn't have the right answer and it was easy to fall in love with what I thought was the right thing to do. Understanding that leading by asking questions and fixing things through other people was key to overcome the mistakes. It's not possible to have all the answers, particularly in today's world. You must be comfortable with ambiguity and learn how to collaborate more. Through my mistakes I also learnt that inclusion = commitment.

What personal qualities do you see in the best middle managers?

Leadership and management is all about what you **consistently do** on a day to day basis. It's all about your rituals and routines. Like all great success stories, it requires **discipline**. I believe leaders and middle managers in today's digital age should focus on:

Discipline 1: Creating a high-performance environment where success is inevitable

Discipline 2: Awakening possibility in people to deliver extraordinary

results
    Discipline 3: Operating with boldness, simplicity and speed
    Discipline 4: Striving to be 100% Authentic
    Discipline 5: Inspiring Action
    Discipline 6: Creating High Performance Teams
    Discipline 7: Unleashing Innovation
    Discipline 8: Managing Ambiguity and Risk
    Discipline 9: Educating People
    Discipline 10: Delivering at Pace

What skills do you think middle managers should focus on developing to ensure their effectiveness over their career?

Top skills for me are resiliency, facilitation, working with groups, meetings, problem solving, collaboration, strategic thinking, team-building, story-telling, emotional intelligence, empathy, conflict resolution, courageous conversations, influencing, coaching, mentoring, listening, agile working, project and change leadership (including stakeholder management).

What do you know now that you wish you knew as a middle manager?

You are 100% responsible what happens and what doesn't happen to you. You are in total control of how you respond to any situation. Standards drive performance improvement. Life is a journey. Do what you think is right. Fear is fun in disguise. Have fun! Remember why you are doing what you do. Purpose is key. Balance strategy with culture. The planning process is more important that the plan.

What's your Tip for the Top?

Strive to be 100% authentic and build your emotional intelligence

What is the one book you would recommend to every middle manager?

That's easy – Leadership Laid Bare!

What two things have struck you most from what was said?

What one thing will you do differently/employ as a result of what you've learnt from this chapter?

9

John Thomson, OBE

Brigadier, British Army; Deputy Lieutenant of Cheshire

John Thomson joined the Army in 1973 after a brief job in as a bank clerk. After a long and happy career in the Army, he became a teacher and after retiring from that in 2012, he became managing director of his wife's child care business.

What was your best memory or achievement as a middle manager?

I think, first, it's probably a good idea to define middle management in the military context. For me that would probably be as a captain or a major. As a company commander, I was starting to receive responsibility for 100-plus people, to do a specific task well. I was responsible for their welfare, I was responsible for their recruiting, I was responsible for, in some respects, their family as well. I'm a big believer in family life.

I think I went to a quite difficult company, which was quite fragmented. Full of good soldiers, but lacking direction maybe. And within six months we were on top form, everybody was enthusiastic, and, then I was thinking: "What's next?" We had a good family life, so we had the families coming in on family days, and guys dressing up as Father Christmas, and all the rest of it. So as a whole package, I felt that we had created something that was to benefit not just me as company commander, but to everybody.

When I look back now, it's interesting that one of my responsibilities as a commander is to develop people. I'm responsible, not just for ticking them on the register, but I'm responsible for their training, their welfare, and all the rest of the things I mentioned. Part of that is looking at their career structure and preparing them for promotion, for their next job. And maybe the job after that as well, because that's the way the Army works. It talent spots early, and develops early. So, we have this natural progression and desire to see people succeed.

What are one or two things you did to get this brilliant bunch of soldiers that were going in the wrong direction, united and in the same direction in six months?

You can get into the depths of theatre of leadership here. But in that situation a large part was setting a personal example. You literally had to lead from the front to just get the momentum up.

Once the momentum was running and people were on the move, you then could fall back a bit and talk to individuals and build their confidence to step up to plate. But at the end of the day, they had to feel that they were good at what they did. So, it was a question of personal example, you're a soldier, you should be fit, can shoot, and you look like a soldier. You build their capability.

But at the same time, what follows on behind that, and this is the real oil in the engine, is recognition. When they become recognised as being good at what they do, that's where you achieve a momentum.

Who was the best boss or commander you ever had and why?

I've had lots of really good commanders, but one does stand out. It was when I first joined the Cheshire Regiment. I came from the Royal Welch Fusiliers to the Cheshire's on a posting. I met a colonel called Philip Wilde, who was the first commanding officer of the 3rd Battalion, which had been formed. This man led by personal example, he had integrity, he had honesty, and he had capability. When you've got all those things, the one lesson I learned from him was how he could motivate people by just spending time talking to them.

The danger is, when you've got all those things, you must be aware of, what I think the New Zealanders call, the "tall poppy syndrome". He left the Army as a lieutenant colonel. To me, he should have left the Army as a four-star general. He had everything in place. When you looked at him you saw a soldier. When you looked at him you saw capability. He was approachable. If you made a mistake, well, he obviously on occasions voiced his displeasure but did it in such a way that there was an education cycle in that as well.

So, you were never going to make that mistake again. To me, he had it all. Superbly fit man, so if he wanted to be, he would be at the front of the runs. But often he would drop back and encourage people at the back, and then run back to the front. The whole thing about the leadership role is, to me, about integrity. And he had it all.

What was the greatest challenge you faced as a captain and major?

When you get to captain/major some people will stop there. I think my challenge was a personal one in the fact that I think I had to achieve a clarity of purpose. "What exactly was it I wanted to be?" It's no good saying, "I want to be the boss", if you're saying that simply because you want the position. I'm very keen on people identifying, their own glass ceiling. I knew where I wanted to go to, and I knew what I want to do when I got there.

So, I think my own personal challenge was refining that viewpoint. But also refining this issue of, having decided that my viewpoint was, I wanted to take responsibility for situations and soldiers. It was also to make sure that I had the skills to do that. So sometimes it was a question of observation from people like Philip Wilde. Just watching how he conducted himself was an education. He was a good tutor. And other times it was a question of throwing yourself in at the deep end, which Philip Wilde did to me. He sent me on the All Arms Tactics Course, as a very young officer.

First of all, I was thinking, "I'm going to sink without a trace here." But then when I thought about it, he wouldn't have sent me there if I was going to sink without a trace. He believed I could do it. So it was that integrity thing again. And I think that, to me, was probably the most salient one. I decided what I wanted to do, and I wanted to make sure I'd got the skills to do it.

What was the biggest mistake you made when you were in that captain / major position?

Failure and mistakes. Always interesting, these two words, because they're viewed as terminal in the UK.

Somebody fails at their business, it's perceived as a shocking thing to carry. You made a terrible mistake there, it was shocking. To me, failure is a steppingstone to success, as long as you use it for the right reason. You learn better after a failure. My personal failure was when I was a captain, I think. I learnt that ego is a huge destroyer of integrity.

I was responsible for something. I was told to do something which I didn't agree with, because it would have brought harm to the people I was commanding. It was a team that ran across mountains. We were told to get to a certain position on a mountain one day, which was extremely dangerous, and I refused to do it. And I went head-to-head with the Major, and of course, you can guess what happened. He sacked me. Why was that a mistake on my part? It could have damaged my career. As it happens, it didn't. But somebody else took over, and they did what they were told, and one of the soldiers got very badly injured.

Now, it was a mistake on my part, because I let my ego get in the way. What I should have done is to manage that situation. I should have said,

"Very good, sir." And when I got to that point on the hill when I decided it was too dangerous, I could then change the plan. So, the mistake was not understanding myself better. It's all very well standing on high and telling people what you're not going to do, but sometimes it leads to a situation which is exactly the opposite that you want to create.

And you've lost control of that then because you haven't got the ability to influence it.

You're on the side-line. That, to me, was a lesson I learned, and it's a lesson I have often pointed out to young offices as well. "Beware. I understand you've got to establish yourself as a young officer. You've got an audience in your soldiers. They all want to think they're commanded by John Wayne. But don't perform. If you've got something to say, you say it in private, and you rationalise it.

I should have led, and I should have got to the point where it got dangerous, and then said, "No, we can't do this." Because nobody else would have been around to say, "You must." So, I'd have come down off the hill a different way. I'm not saying I wouldn't have said to the soldiers, "If anybody asks, we did it." But the manner in which I handled that, I let my ego get in the way. That was a huge lesson.

Ego is the enemy, especially with rank. Rank and position. If you analyse lots of people who pick up positions of power, they change. When I picked up command of the battalion, one of the staff officers said, "Well, I know your style, sir, you'll have to change now." But I said, "I've got here because I am doing what I do, so I'm not going to change." If you change to a point where your ego is more important to you than the purpose that you're supposed to fulfil, you've lost control again.

What personal qualities do you see in the best middle managers, captains or majors?

We'll park capability for a minute, because we can assume, they're capable, that's why they've got there. We'll take that as a given. I think honesty, is a characteristic that I respect in people. **Openness, approachability, sincerity** in the fact that they are there to be a force for good. They're not there for themselves. The best commanders I've ever come across they have those things in buckets. They were clearly very capable men, but they had it in buckets full.

One of the best bosses I ever worked for was a woman. Society has got this tussle between male/female, young/old, and all the rest of it. This was a woman that had all those things I've just mentioned in spades. She was a real force for good for a lot of young people because of her honesty and her integrity. Sometimes she would stand up for what she felt was right, which might not have been career clever. But she was an excellent, excellent leader. So, it's nothing to do with being male or female, or the captain image - with a bayonet clamped between your teeth and "follow me" - sometimes it's a bit of sharpness.

I'm a big believer in emotional intelligence. Reading people, understanding where they are, and therefore, what you should do to bring them on and not knock them back. These people had that before somebody invented the term emotional intelligence. They just could read people. Probably because they've been there. And that's where a lot of my ability comes from. I recognise where I've come from and what that's given me, and I'm not going to ignore it because there's some mileage in that when I'm dealing with other people. I can see a transfer that helps me to understand that person.

Sometimes when you chastise somebody, it may have to be a wagging finger, other times it might be a hand on the shoulder. You've got to read the situation. One size does not fit all. Certainly, in business, where I find when people are striving for efficiency, they strive for one size fits all. Well, I've got a conflict between efficiency and effectiveness. One size doesn't fit all. You've got to be sensitive to each individual situation, to each individual person. You are responsible for moving it on, you're not just responsible for judging it. I don't judge people, I conduct an estimate, which gives me the wherewithal to decide how I'm going to go on to help that person. So, it's not a question of judging, it's a question of assisting.

What skills do you think middle managers should focus on developing to ensure their effectiveness over their career?

Strangely enough, I'd say, "Associate with the right people".

I don't mean necessarily people higher up the chain of command. It could well be people below the chain of command. I got a lot of information, intelligence, by sitting on my helmet in Iraq, surrounded by a few guys, drinking out of this disgusting army tea mug and listening. So, one of the key skills for me is listening. People make a throwaway comment, and you say, "I'm not sure where that fits just now, but I'll log it." You don't put it away.

So, I think most certainly listening. What I mean by associating with the right people, is understanding the people you are responsible for commanding. I have an issue with command and control. In certain circumstances soldiers expect it, so you should deliver on it. But for general purposes I'm more in the General McChrystal style of command.

General Stan McChrystal was in Iraq, early 2003. His brilliance was in understanding people, getting people to mesh, bringing their skills, individual skills, to the table. Well, you can only do that if you've made an assessment, and you can only make an assessment through listening. And we don't listen enough today. When you watch a conversation, you will see somebody talking, and the person they're talking to is getting ready to launch on the response.

Conversational listening, I call it, not active listening.

That person you're actually chatting to will pick up on the fact you are listening to respond, and he will see it as a dishonest.

That ability to tailor a conversation, a true conversation, where you take what's being said to you and then you deliver that back is priceless.

Making assumptions when you're in a position of responsibility is where people go wrong. Sometimes you have to make a quick assumption, which you then should test against your previous knowledge, and test maybe more specific. But just taking the throwaway assessments into an assumption is clearly wrong.

So, to me, listening is a skill, as it communicating, speaking people's language. My father, who was a soldier, used to say to me, "You should be able to speak to princes and paupers as a young officer." That's a skill I try to refine. I was a Fusilier when I first joined, I was a private. The Army gave me a commission. When I speak to Lance Corporal Jones 36, I wouldn't speak to him in any different way than I'd speak to General what's-his-face. That doesn't mean to say that I leave corporal 36 behind, I speak his language. I don't see the necessity in upgrading my language when I speak to the general.

I used to say to young staff officers, "When I write a paper it should be able to be read by a Lance Corporal, private soldier, and a General." So, write to express, not to impress. It's the same with verbal communication.

When you speak to somebody, it's a question of expression, it's not a question of trying to impress them with who you are, your position, because that's where everything falls apart. To resurrect that conversation to anything that's got to be meaningful is going to be extremely difficult and has to be in the hands of a very capable individual. So, I would say those are the three areas that I would focus on.

What do you know now that you wish you knew as a middle manager?

When I used to go to the Staff College to present to young majors who all want to be generals this time next week this is the question that always came up, "If you knew then, sir, what you know now, what would you change?" And the answer is I'm not sure I would change it a huge amount. To some degree I'm a fatalist. Things happen for a reason sometimes. The other thing is, worry about the things you can change, don't worry about the things you can't change.

I would also say not to be afraid of failure. Everybody is frightened stiff about failing, so they hide failure. And by hiding it they don't make use of it.

As an example, I was sent on the All Arms Tactics Course, as a young officer, and you have to go on TEWTs, (tactical exercises without troops). And you stand on a hill somewhere, looking at the piece of real estate in front of you, with maps. They say, "The 13th Motor Rifle Regiment from the Soviet Union's coming towards you, what's your plan?"

Everybody in the group got asked except me. And every time I tried to answer I was met with a "Thanks for that", and the instructor would ask somebody else.

So, I was thinking, "Is this guy protecting me because he thinks I'm a numpty?" So later on that evening I went to see him, Major Rory Gilchrist, Black Watch was his name, and asked why. He looked perplexed and confused by my question and said, "I don't understand."

I asked, "Why are you blocking me? Is it because you think I'm going to get it wrong and make a fool of myself?" He said, "No, why would I ask a question in a group like that to a person that I know knows the answer." So suddenly I've gone from one mindset to another about my abilities.

That's the type of thing that holds up children's education, and holds up people's careers, by wondering, "I don't think I'm up to that." Our job as either commanders or middle leaders, whatever you call it, our job is to release that potential and reduce this fear of failure.

To find a way for each individual to release it, because it's a waste otherwise. I used to worry about mates of mine who went into the pit. They were in the pit five years, pits closed down, they went on to the industrial estate. Later on, in life they started to say, "Well, why don't I stop doing this? I'm going to train to become a plumber." And now they run their own plumbing businesses. We could have taken 20 years off that journey. And that's where I think the major contribution is for the middle manager, is to facilitate that.

I wished I'd known more about the ethos of the Army, which is to prepare people under your command to effectively eventually overtake you. I didn't understand that, I thought it was "dog eat dog" when you first arrive. But people were there trying to prepare me to one day get promoted. And I have. I've outranked now a good proportion of the people who trained and led me.

It was because of their efforts though. And if I'd have understood that a bit more, I could have maybe made more use of it than I did.

Some years ago Iceland foods invited me to be their keynote speaker at their conference. And they were looking at performance and the title of the conference was: 'We're going to war'.

When I got there they were all in plastic helmets and camouflage. What they wanted was to win back their market share. That was their war. I was sharing a story about, when I was a commanding officer part of my responsibility was to manage the careers of those who were company commanders and majors. And at some point, everybody wants to command their battalion, but sometimes I may have to tell somebody that, "I'm sorry, you're not going to be able to do that."

"So, I have to write you down. I'm not going to recommend you for command. However, I am going to recommend you for something else. And the chances are, you'll overtake me, because you'll be a round peg in a round hole."

"I understand the joy of commanding a battalion, but what I'm saying to you is, unfortunately you're not going to get there. You just don't have that skill." And it's the hardest thing you'll probably ever have to do, but it is the right thing.

I used to say to my young officers, "Remember, always do the proper thing, not the popular thing." Because if I then put that person forward for the job and then he crashes and burns. His career is finished. It's gone. And that's because I was dishonest with him. An act of cowardice almost, because I didn't have the moral credence to say, "I'm sorry, I don't think you can do that." That's the hard bit.

That's where the whole issue of your position as a leader, a middle manager, call it what you will, there are responsibilities that you cannot shirk. Lots of people do, but they do it to their cost, and to the cost of the organisation as well.

What's your one Tip for the Top?

Well, getting to the top I'd say, "Be yourself, be honest". I think the second thing I would say, "Don't think about what the job can give you but think about what you can bring to the job."

So, imagine you command a battalion, someone under your command might ask, "Well, I've had lots of commanding officers before, what's going to be different about your command? What are you going to bring to that battalion that's going to add to its colour, to the quality of its life?" Think hard about that and find it.

Often when you find it you realise it's the trigger point, it's the very thing that takes people to the next level. So, they might be operating at a satisfactory level here, and everybody smiles at each other, and they feel okay. But once you discover what that is, then everybody goes to the next level.

That changes the momentum of the cycle. So, once you've triggered that, you find then that your momentum of change gets quicker because people are enthusiastic for it. They don't distrust change.

I think it's what you can bring to the job just as much as what the job can bring to you, whether it's fancy stars on your shoulders, or a bigger house, or whatever it might be. Think hard about that, because that's where the real return on that job will come to you.

The fact that you've got fancy stars on your shoulders is okay, and if you behave yourself and you keep your head below the parapet, you don't do anything wrong, you might get some more. But the real satisfaction is knowing that you've done a proper job.

When I left the battalion, I realised that my job was to ensure that after I left it went on to greater things. A lot of people, because of their ego, would say, "Oh, it's probably going to collapse after I leave because I've gone." That's irresponsible. You develop people behind you, and you bring that to the job. You get right people in the right places. After you've gone, after six months, who are you? There's a new commanding officer in place and he's doing a great job.

I had this conversation with my son. He was commissioned straight from school. It's interesting to see how the different generations see things. I'm interested in knowing more about millennial's, because they're the ones coming into the workforce now, in greater numbers. I think there's a different approach needed.

In some cases, it's got to be almost like a grandfather approach. In other ways, it's got to be correcting some of the ills actually. This idea of, "Right. It's my right to have this." You're going to be disappointed, because you ain't going to get it. So how can I avoid that? I can avoid that by modifying their outlook and getting people to look in the right direction. Because it is going to lead to disaster, if you're of the opinion, "This is my right, why haven't I got it?" Eventually, not only will you not get it, you'll not get a lot of other things as well.

What is the one book you'd recommend to every middle manager?

That's a really good question. I'll mention two books, and I'll refine it, which one I would choose in the end. Because there are two. There's a book called The Power of Character, written by a young man called Andrew Reay. He is an Ex-RAF officer, who is currently working in education.

He's looked at questions such as: 'What should education be? How we should approach children? How we should enable children? What atmosphere do we bring children up in?' It's well worth a read, because I think he's probably seizing on the right things. He is at the King's Leadership Academy in Warrington, who are demonstrating they've got it right. They've got some real characters in the school, and they're getting exceptional results. And it's no accident, it's their approach. I'm positive of that.

The other one is General Stan McChrystal's book, Team of Teams. And the reason why I cite Team of Teams, is because this is part of that evaluation process that everybody should go into and not make assumptions.

Every army has a standing operating procedure, the way that they go about things. Sometimes that can straight-jacket you, and it can also make you predictable as well. For example, the old Soviet forces, they had a doctrine, I could predict what was coming next. So, if you can predict it, you can counter it.

McChrystal's took over a situation in Afghanistan ... Iraq first, and then Afghanistan and it was a different type of warfare. You might hear people talking about 'asymmetric warfare'. They don't play fair. They don't wear different uniforms to us so we can identify them. They don't stand in rank, shoulder to shoulder, and advance across the battlefield anymore. It's unfair, it's not right. They shoot and scoot. So, from shooting you one minute the next minute they're hoeing the fields. You don't know who they are.

So, he realised that he had to modify his approach. And this meant that we have to have SOPs, (standard operating procedures) and they're for routine things. But for the manner in which we go about business means you really need to empower junior commanders. So, they haven't got to report back and say, "I've just come across an armoured car, sir. What do I do?" You say to them, "Look, I'm going to give you the picture." Good commanders are good storytellers, they put the visual picture in your mind. So, "That's what I want to achieve, fellas, okay?"

When you get to your area of responsibility and you encounter something, think of the picture. So you take whatever action you want to. It's called mission command in military speak. You interpret what you see, you fulfil my intent, but you command your battle. So it becomes truly, not your battle, not my battle, but our battle, because I've enabled you.

The FBI, CIA, are not renowned for getting on with each other. McChrystal's ability was to break down the silos between organisations like the Green Berets, the Seals. He recognised that everyone had something to bring to the party. This created an ability to increase the "speed of manoeuvre", he could outpace the enemy now. He could virtually be there before they were. He could respond to something they are showing before they did. It was a very intelligent way of doing it.

When you read the book you realise it was his personality that brought it about. He was a four-star general who didn't stand at the front and say, "I'm the boss, listen very carefully." He actually moved amongst people. He synthesised them into a team, and every one of them were teams in their own right. It's a good lesson on evaluating, one, the task; two, the people, and three, the myriad of capabilities that you have. Having done that, you've got to ask yourself the question, "So what process do I need to form one team which is going to counter the problem?" Whichever it is, whether it's business or whether it's warfare. It's a very good read indeed.

I think Power of Character is for the future. It's for setting foundations now, that we'll see the benefit of in time. But as of today, if you are taking over a new job, maybe with turning around a company that's failing, Team of Teams would be a good starting point.

What question haven't I asked that you think I should have?

I think it's the "why" question. Why do people do this? Why do people strive to become middle managers or commanders, or whatever it is? I did it because I've always wanted to know where my ceiling is. So, I've tested myself in various ways, and a lot of them resulted in physical pain as well. But knowing your boundaries, identifying your boundaries, and then begging the question, "What do I need to do to cross that boundary?"

What two things have struck you most from what was said?

What one thing will you do differently/employ as a result of what you've learnt from this chapter?

10

Sandra McDowell

Customer Engagement Director, Kin+Carta.

Kin+Carta Connect is a 180-strong digital marketing agency, with offices in Manchester, London, Liverpool, Edinburgh and Chicago.

So what was your best memory or achievement when you were in that kind of middle-management spectrum?

When you work for an agency, you play two roles. The first is nurturing talent and delivering profit for your agency while the second is doing great work for your clients. The reflection I want to share is about a project that transformed the client's business: those opportunities rarely come along which is why it's stuck in my mind. It was a big corporate and they'd asked us to handle some internal comms work while they were short staffed. My biggest achievement was when the chief executive asked me to develop internal and external communications strategies and completely restructure his team. His belief in me was infectious. I thought I was quite good at my communication skills, but he witnessed something in me that I didn't see in myself.

This CEO just had utter belief in me. It was incredible. What he wanted to build was a corporate function with a consumer agency mind-set. He wanted people like me who had an insatiable desire to do a better job, to be proactive and to be action oriented. He needed a culture where you didn't rest on your laurels. I started to fulfil his brief, but it wasn't plain sailing. He was so difficult to work for because he demanded 110%. I'd come out of some meetings exasperated by him, but because I knew he believed in me I kept going, rather giving in.

Actually, the traits that he was craving are the traits that transfer into any business. They are about productivity and action orientation. I think the lesson I learned from this experience is set the bar as high as you can. Demand perfection; strive to be the best you can and never lower your standards.

Who was the best boss you've ever had, and why?

It was Natalie Gross at Amaze. Natalie and I were very different in our areas of professional expertise and our personal style. We got on most of the time but sometimes didn't see eye to eye. So while not an utterly harmonious relationship we learned to respect one another.

The first lesson I learned from Nat was how to work with someone whose personal chemistry was so different to mine. She was an introvert. Sometimes the interpersonal skills of an introvert are hard to interpret. She would have a demeanour that was hard to read and her words never revealed what she meant. You just had to unravel it stage by stage. As a consequence, I did a lot of research into personality types and techniques to build a better rapport with the various traits people hold (but don't always display). It's a vital skill for business as well as in personal life.

But ultimately, she gained my respect because of the way she thought. Actually, I think that's what I admire the most about her. She is a real thinker. She has an innate ability to flip your point of view on its head and help you see it from a different perspective. Looking back it was incredible to have somebody in my midst who'd think for a minute, sit quietly, pause and then ask me to look at the situation we were trying to unravel another way. She never gave me the answer, rather an approach to problem solving. That bigger picture thinking was probably her strongest trait.

I think that realisation has influenced my management style. I always try and take a step back and do a bit more thinking before I speak. The pause technique that she used was her natural style, which I've learned to adopt. When you witness it, it is very strong.

What was the greatest challenge you faced as a middle manager?

This is quite a tough one. I think one of the frustrations I had as a middle manager was that I saw my boss getting recognition or acknowledgement that was undeserved. That was a big problem for me because in some instances, the work this person was taking credit for was my work. So I got frustrated. I felt I couldn't respect my boss because he wasn't adopting the same value set as me.

I had two choices either put up with it or, build the courage to get myself noticed. I took it upon myself just to speak to senior people more often in the corridor and wander into their offices for a chat. I made sure that the senior people knew what the team and I were achieving. Slowly, they started to recognise who was doing the work long before a report was submitted.

I think when you're in that middle management layer, you're probably a good technical person or craftsman because that's what you've been taught to do. If you want to gain greater recognition, don't hide behind your specialism. That was a lesson that I learned, simply finding a way to just influence people by being yourself and being human. And most senior people are smart enough to see. You don't need a veneer, be authentic and do your own PR.

What would you advise female readers; women in careers in that middle management sector in terms of getting a coach?

I have learned that women often suffer from imposter syndrome. We worry about whether we can do a job which holds us back from even trying. Meanwhile men just give it a go and achieve well – because they haven't talked themselves out of it.

To help me get over my imposter syndrome, I just needed somebody to help me with my confidence. I used a career coach, but the techniques she was teaching me were about how to understand what's important to me in the first instance. Coaching often is about teasing out what people can't articulate by themselves, so my advice is to find time for yourself to do some bigger thinking. I've been so busy being a career person, being a mum, being a wife, being a friend, and neglected to find time to do any real thinking about me and where I'm heading.

What was the biggest mistake you made when you were in middle management?

I don't know if I can be as specific as a single mistake I made in middle management, so my reflection is about my career path. I didn't have a plan. I'd find a job I liked the sound of, go for the interview, get the job, and then I make the job my own. I seemed more comfortable with spotting opportunities for myself within the business rather than moving around a lot. I've actually done quite a lot with my career but it just happened rather than being designed by me.

When I'm coaching people now, I try to help them map where they're going. You don't need to know exactly which jobs you need to be doing, but it is good to have an idea of the things you need to learn to become fluent in, versus the things that make you happy.

My mistake, if you can call it that, is staying too long in any one job. Even though you might be progressing in your career, new environments teach you new skills - and these develop you as an individual – allowing you to become adaptable to change.

What personal qualities do you see in the best middle managers?

There are three qualities that I admire:

The first is **ambition**. I admire people who know what they want to achieve and set goals to help them get there. Particularly, as I work at an agency, you can be busy in meetings all day and actually not deliver all the things that you want to do. Set out the things you want for yourself within your role, so you're able to reflect on an achievement when you've delivered it.

Having a point of view is my second. Often middle managers lack the confidence or knowledge to speak up in front of senior colleagues. However, if you do your homework, craft an opinion on a topic you're passionate about and find the platform to voice your opinion you can build your confidence. The more you put well-reasoned arguments forward, the more others will seek your opinion out.

The third quality I admire is **honesty** of approach. I have come across so many people with high levels of self-confidence who're unable to admit when they're wrong. There is something very powerful in holding your hands up to a client or customer. You haven't tried to back yourself out of it. You haven't tried to blame others. You have admitted you've made a mistake. This approach has worked in my favour. If a client is being particularly aggressive to you and you admit that you're wrong, the aggression dissipates. Then you can start to rebuild the relationship.

What skills do you think middle managers should focus on developing to ensure their focus over their career?

I don't know whether it's a skill or it's a trait, but having an insatiable appetite for learning is my big thing.

You can't be effective in your career if you don't put the effort in. You can't go to your boss and ask for a promotion unless you've demonstrated that you're what that boss needs. It's not just doing the job you're being paid to do either. It's thinking outside the job. It's reading things, spotting opportunities. It's reflecting on what you've seen and having an opinion.

So when digital came along I thought I'm not going to get left behind here. This is the new thing and I need to learn about it, understand it. So even now, I'm still always reading avidly and sharing things that inspire me. My brain is full. I'm not an expert by any means, because it moves so quickly, but if you don't stay in tune with what's going on you'll quickly get left behind.

So that kind of desire, that hunger is what I admire most. I can name people here who work alongside me who have that insatiable appetite and it delights me. They want to do well themselves, they want to continue their learning. They want to be a success and that means delivering exceptional work for our clients.

What do you now know that you wish you knew then?

I think I said it earlier, it's taking time to just think. Freud said 'the years of struggle will strike you as the most beautiful.' My take on that is to learn from the negative moments in your life, because actually you'll get gain more from that those experiences than you will the successes. So take a little bit of time out to just reflect on you and your behaviours. It teaches you to become more self-aware.

What's your one tip for the top then?

Keep asking 'why?' Not everybody thinks they have the ability to be strategic, but a strategist is a thinker. The more you ask why and put challenges in front of yourself, the better you'll be at navigating life.

And, if I can add a second tip. Understand what 'the top' means. Set your own measures of success. Is it about seniority in management? Deep expertise can be just as valuable and often more rewarding.

What two things have struck you most from what was said?

What one thing will you do differently/employ as a result of what you've learnt from this chapter?

11

Jaki Salisbury

Former CFO, CX & Non Exec Board Director, Public Sector; Management Consultant

Jaki is a former Finance Director with several local authorities. She took on the role of Chief Executive of a rapidly growing District Council before becoming Interim Chief Executive responsible for setting up and running a new Unitary Council in 2009 – a huge project achieved in just 9 months – it was a merger of 60% of a County Council and two District Councils. She is now a widely respected management consultant, working mainly with local authorities, to help develop senior leadership talent and teams and helps Councils work through difficult challenges. Mentoring senior managers now forms a large part of her work.

What was your best memory or achievement as a middle manager?

I was working at a lean, district council in my first real management role, and despite what lots of people think, there are many well-run councils. We were a very business-like council, very conscious of our costs and customers. We were one of three councils nationally, jointly developing and implementing a new financial management system with McDonnell Douglas Information Systems, a huge corporation. For us, this was a big project with big resource implications. Everyone had to deliver their normal work, as well as do all the testing and development and we were a very lean team to start with. The new system hadn't been set up as a special project and wasn't resourced as a project, which was a big learning point for the future.

The achievement was getting everybody working really well together, and delivering, despite the huge workloads. People worked evenings and weekends for many, many months in order to develop the system, get it working and actually deliver on the council's investment. We were able to get a great team feeling, despite the adversity, or probably because of it! The team was very agile and flexible and we managed to keep a good sense of humour. There was a real can-do attitude and problems were overcome together. My main role throughout this period was to keep the team focused on the big picture and to try and ensure we didn't get bogged down. I felt like a spinner of plates, keeping an oversight of everything but delegating to others and trying to intervene only when needed. We had everyone pulling together in the same direction with a clear goal and agreed priorities. Leadership from everyone resulted in a great team spirit and innovative ideas. With this approach you can achieve your goals even with limited resources.

I raised my concerns with senior management that this should have been set up and resourced as a special project and that we needed some extra resources to finish the project. I also said that individual efforts over and above the norm should be recognised. This was challenging as it wasn't the norm in that organisation but I felt a responsibility to the team. I was able to bring some extra resources into the team, and get some recompense for the additional hours. People don't necessarily need monetary reward to feel valued, but in this instance it demonstrated that the organisation recognised the huge efforts of the team in going way above and beyond what could reasonably be expected.

Who was the best boss you ever had and why?

There was one senior manager who gave me the opportunity and support to move up from being a middle manager leading a relatively small finance team, into a senior management role leading several larger teams, covering a number of diverse functions.

It meant I leapt over my immediate boss to get the role, having already being promoted over my previous boss, so I am grateful to both the councillors and the senior manager who recognised my passion and enthusiasm and were prepared to give me a chance. I was in my late 20's at the time, so it was a huge opportunity.

Another thing he did was to send me on a five-day, off-site, experiential leadership course. This was run by Cipfa, my accountancy institute, to help move people from being good technical managers to become effective people managers and senior leaders. It was life changing, not just work wise but personally too. It enabled me to understand why I am like I am and my preferred management style. I am a right brained person which is fairly unusual for a qualified accountant and helps to explain why my focus has always been on people.

So that was really, really helpful and started my interest in management development. I was, and still am, passionate about trying to support every individual to develop themselves and their teams, to push boundaries and comfort zones so that we all achieve our potential.

What was the greatest challenge you faced as a middle manager?

Understanding that others did not think like I did and did not see the world in the same way was initially a big challenge for me. One of the things I found out is that I think and behave quite differently to other people and from the personality assessments my results were not the usual combinations. For example, I was willing to take risks in a very risk averse world. I had to make sure I treated people as individuals as a blanket approach would not work.

As I moved into a senior management role it became more important for me to understand how other people think and understand how my preferred style impacts on others, particularly more junior members of the team. I tend to think out loud, want to discuss things and then come to a conclusion and a course of action. I am happy for everyone to just throw their thoughts in but didn't realise that perhaps some people didn't feel they could. Also, this approach may not be very helpful to some people who perhaps need time to reflect. I needed to be clear about how other people operated and how they thought, and try and make sure that I changed my style in order for them to receive the information in a clear way for them. I found that quite hard, especially to begin with – I had to be careful not to "run over" people and their thoughts with my passion and excitement about what it was we were doing and my views about how we should do it.

What was the biggest mistake you made when you were a middle manager?

I think it comes partly from the greatest challenge, because I naively assumed that everyone wanted change to deliver improvements as much as I did. I always remember from an early training session the phrase ASSUME makes an ASS out of U and ME. To me it was such a no-brainer to try and improve processes, to streamline the way we do things – especially for our customers – in our case the taxpayer - to save time, to cut costs, and also develop people to be the best they could be. I wanted to enjoy my job, and I wanted everybody to enjoy their job as much as they could.

I assumed we would all just get on with doing the best we could for ourselves, the team, and the organisation. It was a bit of a shock to realise that not everybody thinks like that. Some people saw no reason to improve things even if it made the whole process more efficient and saved money. Some in fact resisted change, making the whole process more difficult and time consuming and others became "terrorists" causing problems and delays. The question is then how do you take people with you? The answer is to understand where individuals are coming from, their issues and concerns and what motivates them. I also learnt it was important to involve people from the beginning and to try and quantify the benefits to them as individuals. It was also about recognising that sometimes the right place for them is not in their current role and if their values are not the same as the organisation's then it is probably time for them to look elsewhere.

What personal qualities do you see in the best middle managers?

Integrity is absolutely key, because otherwise we do not gain the trust of our people. It took me 2/3 years in one council to gain everyone's trust as the previous incumbent had not done what they said they would. It took a while for people to realise that I did mean what I said and I would do what I said. You have to earn people's trust and respect – don't assume that people will believe you just because you are the manager.

Passion and a positive can do attitude are important as passion helps you sell the vision and get the team spirit going and a can do attitude makes a huge difference to achieving success.

Self-awareness and self-management - You've got to have this before you can manage a team. You need to be able to manage yourself, know your strengths and weaknesses and be able to prioritise and deliver. Understand that 80/20 is good enough and don't allow yourself to procrastinate.

Be self-confident and see the big picture and what needs to be done, and don't get bogged down in the detail.

Leadership and influencing skills are essential and we have to keep developing these as we go through our career. Get feedback and use coaches and mentors to keep challenging and developing yourself.

Be realistic, not optimistic and **communicate fully all the time**. Too often things fail or are harder than they need to be as unrealistic and optimistic plans are made or resources not fully considered. People always seem to say it will be easier next year, but it won't, there will just be a different set of issues to resolve. If we don't communicate what's happening others will fill the void with their own version of the truth.

Be innovative and also caring when finding solutions – there are always options available to us when we are trying to resolve an issue. Being positive and focusing on possible solutions is essential and we should always bear in mind the impact of our preferred solutions on individuals and teams and involve them in the process. I like the saying its nice to be important but its more important to be nice.How we behave as managers has a big impact on others – it is up to us to ensure it is positive not negative.

What skills do you think middle managers should focus on developing to ensure their effectiveness over their career?

Dealing with people well, great communication and delivery on time and to budget – under promise and over deliver, not the other way round.

People – for me it all revolves around people, and at the end of the day, if you have a switched on, enthusiastic and determined team, you can achieve almost anything. I believe we demonstrated that when we launched the new Unitary Authority - because we did what was almost impossible in just nine months.

Communication - As human beings, we seem to be inherently bad at communicating. This applies both within the organisation and with our customers hence the saying you can never communicate enough. One thing I learnt was that if I didn't say anything as a senior manager that people would make things up. They would fill the void with their own version of the truth.

I'd hear comments saying "I know we're doing X, Y, and Z, but nobody's heard anything for a while, so you ought to know they're now assuming A, B, and C." To me that didn't make any sense, but that's what happens. And that's why communication, together with empathy and an understanding of what makes people tick is so important.

Delivery – To under promise and over deliver is so simple and so effective. Also, as a manager you have to grasp the nettles - if you've got someone who is not performing as they should, it needs to be addressed. They may be a square peg in a round hole, and they may have some great skills, but unless you can give them something that utilises those great skills and is going to make them happy and give them job satisfaction, then it's not going to work. The challenge is to spot that and help them and the organisation get the most from their talent.

What do you know now that you wish you knew as a middle manager?

I was a middle manager in the 80's, aka the macho 80's. One of the things I now say to people is that it's a strength and not a weakness to admit that you don't know it all, and that you can't do it all.This shows maturity and honesty but you do need to come up with options.

This is particularly true if you've only got enough resources to do part of what it is you've been asked to do. A mature and effective manager doesn't work every night and every weekend trying to do more and more themselves, or cover for Jill or Jack, or whoever. They have their head up, are clear about saying "given the resources and given the priorities, we need to really major on this, this and this, we need to defer that, that can be left for a bit". They get agreement to the revised priorities and also delegate effectively, adult to adult.

So, although very early on in my career, I felt I did have to have all the answers as well as work long hours, I learnt quite quickly that if I didn't know the answer then it was better to say that and to say I would find out as I knew someone who did. I had a big network so I used my network to help me, which worked really well.

And last but not least – honour our biology - a balance is really important for yourself and everyone in the team! Take time out to eat, sleep and have fun - see family and friends and refresh your brain and body. This delivers perspective as well as greater creativity, productivity and resilience. After all we are human beings.

What's your one Tip for the Top?

That it's all about people so managers must address behaviours, attitudes and performance that aren't in line with the team's values and corporate values otherwise you will never have a great performing team.

If not tackled it becomes permitted, authorised by default, so then it becomes more difficult to change and this impacts on the performance of both the individual and the team. You have to deal with things straight away. Sometimes people have got problems, either at work or at home that they need help with, that affects their behaviour and performance. Sometimes they are not suited to their role, where they are, or they've ended up in a dead-end and they become unhappy and this then affects both them and the team.

What is the one book you'd recommend to every middle manager?

Definitely Crucial Conversations by Kerry Paterson and Joseph Grenny. It's about communication again and also that generally lots of people are worried about having difficult conversations so they avoid grasping the nettle which just means things get worse.

Also the TED talk by Dr Shimi Kang – "What one skill = an awesome life?"

What question haven't I asked that you think I should have?

Who was the worst boss and why?

The worst boss I had who was someone who clocked people back in from lunch, was very inflexible and if you made a mistake you were verbally beat around the head. There was little empathy or understanding and no real interest in individual or team development. It was a very autocratic and blame culture approach.

It didn't make you want to stay at the organisation. It actually changed me from being my normal confident self, into being worried about poor performance, which meant my performance dropped. It becomes a self-fulfilling prophecy and so I left the organisation as soon as I qualified. Luckily had the offer of two jobs and was able to regain my confidence and make rapid progress after leaving, getting my first taste of a Finance Director role in my early 30's.

What two things have struck you most from what was said?

What one thing will you do differently/employ as a result of what you've learnt from this chapter?

12

Julie Meighan

Chief Executive, VMA Group

Julie is the chief executive of VMA Group a recruitment and head-hunting organisation, based in Europe and in Asia. They have a team of 70 that covers and works with every organisation from Fortune 500 companies to a smaller organisations. In the fifteen years since Julie has been running the business, VMA has grown from six to 70 people. She is also an executive coach and works with clients across the globe.

What was your best memory or achievement as a middle manager?

The greatest challenge is one of having empowerment, I think. The problem with middle management is that it's generally A) to get it, and B) to earn it. I think the key thing is understanding what your role is, and how it contributes to the organisation in that form.

What was the biggest mistake you made when you were a middle manager?

I think not getting sufficient ambassadors and support from other key stakeholders. Because you're invisible beyond your own manager.

So, if you don't build a network of key influencers across the organisation who can help you, you can limit your effectiveness. Because it's difficult to get out of there, up or down, or move left or right. You're stuck working for someone that you're largely dependent on because you're in this middle management role.

So unless you have a strategy around how you might network and garner support for who you are and what you're about, outside of your manager, then it's very difficult to get beyond that and to be effective.

What personal qualities do you see in the best middle managers?

Well, the same personal qualities you need in management are, of course, all the way up the ladder. **Self-awareness** is actually critical in today's environment. People all want **authenticity** and **transparency** in terms of your management skills. And you need to be able to build trust and, obviously, that's whether you're a middle manager or a senior manager. You've got to display those qualities.

You have to have an authentic style and to be very authentic in what you need from people and transparent about what you're trying to achieve.

Would you advise middle managers who are serious about their careers, to get their own coach to increase that self-awareness?

I think it's quite difficult for people to achieve that themselves, if it's not something that they have a natural interest in. For those people that haven't developed good levels of emotional intelligence and self-awareness, then I think it's definitely something they need to invest in.

Because ultimately, you need to be able to understand the impact you have on people, whether they're working for you or other stakeholders. You need to be up for developing your skills, which you can only do with a certain amount of self-awareness and reflection.

What skills do you think middle managers should focus on developing to ensure their effectiveness over their career?

Well, let's assume that if you're an ambitious middle manager you're looking to get to the top.

The most highly sought-after skills by any leader in any organisation is someone that is independent thinking and has some vision and creativity, coupled with a natural curiosity.

These are highly sought soft skills in my view and uncommon in middle managers. Too many accept things as a given, they'd rather receive instructions without challenging the status quo.

They're problem solvers, 'problem detectives' in an increasingly complex world. And so, I think problem solving and an ability to be more curious about their organisation is important. How to add value and to challenge of yourself in a cognitive way, without thinking you have to be a 'yes person,'. Too many say "I'm never going to tell the truth, I'm never going to say how I think it is", because they're always worried about repercussions or implications. A good leader needs to be able to say, "I'm going be confident and brave, to stand up and be able to challenge something in a positive non-judgemental way."

What do you know now that you wish you knew as a middle manager?

It's sort of linked to the past, I think what I know now is that people value the ability to challenge and to question things. And I think as a middle manager you don't realise that. You think, you keep your head down and, you just sort of smoothly go along and agree with everything that everyone says, and that somehow, you're going to get more in favour with the bosses. An effective leader today absolutely won't survive without having people that are prepared to challenge and question everything that they're doing and be able to do that internally and externally.

So, if I knew that then, I think I would have been braver and more confident to do that, knowing that it would be well respected. And not be worried about upsetting people, because it's all about how you say things, isn't it? Not what you say.

What's your one Tip for the Top?

I think creating presence and having gravitas goes a long way to getting to the top. In terms of investing in one's self, to build gravitas is all about the ability to build trust and build effective relationships is the thing that I would say that people spend the least amount of time doing. However, the more time they invest in that, the more likely to get to the top.

What is the one book you'd recommend to every middle manager?

Gravitas by Caroline Goyder.

It's a great book and really gives you an insight into what gravitas is, because in my experience a lot of people don't know what gravitas means.

They sort of have preconceived ideas or assumptions about that. But actually, it really is about how you get remembered, how you communicate so that people remember your words and then they actually change behaviour as a result of that. That's about having gravitas.

She also does a great Ted Talk on it as well which I highly recommend people watch.

Who was the best boss you ever had and why?

I've never had a good boss.

I'm afraid you're not going to get much out of me on that one. I've never, ever worked for one, which is why I thought, someday I'm going to work for myself.

Given your experience then of not having a good boss, what's one tip on something that middle managers should absolutely not do if they're serious about moving on in their career?

They shouldn't be judgemental. I think we all find that very difficult to do, but it's about understanding that the potential lies beyond the face value of people. If you have preconceived assumptions and judgements about people, you won't be able to get the best out of them.

You have to believe in everyone, that everyone has potential in the beginning until they tell you otherwise.

What question haven't I asked that you think I should have?

How do you best manage your manager?

You might work for the organisation, but you work for the person that you work for. That's the reason that you might get a promotion or not get a promotion, that's the reason you'll be happy or not happy or have meaning in your job or not meaning in your job. It's a critical aspect and I suppose the question I would ask is how do you best manage your manager for your own personal success, your own personal goals?

The answer is to find out what's important to your manager. Because otherwise you make assumptions about what's important. And you need to build a relationship with that manager to work out what's important to them, you can then make sure that what you're doing is aligned to that

What two things have struck you most from what was said?

What one thing will you do differently/employ as a result of what you've learnt from this chapter?

13

Julian Cobley

Managing Director of the Skills and Growth Company, Cheshire

Julian Cobley has been Managing Director of the Skills and Growth Company since April 2016. The Skills and Growth Company is an arms-length company of Cheshire East Council. Before becoming Managing Director, he was the Head of Investment at the Council where he wrote the business case and the plan to actually create the company.

Julian has held several other roles in local Government as well. He's been the Business Manager of the Economic Growth and Prosperity Directorate working to the Exec Director and before that role's in an IT background and systems development.

He came to public sector in 2007 and prior to that he was in the private sector since he graduated.

What was your best memory or achievement as a middle manager?

I'd probably suggest it was a project I was working on as a middle manager in the Council. It's going back around seven years to 2013 and I was the Head of Business Development in the IT function at the time. My boss at the time came to me and said: 'I think we've got a bit of a problem with broadband connectivity. Can you go away and do a piece of work to just look at it'.

It was one of these activities that was a side of the desk activity, I suppose, to core business. I did investigate it and there was a supply failure. Because of some relationships I had with the telecommunication sector, I was able to formulate a plan to try and address that issue. That led me to securing a significant amount of external funding to deliver that project working with suppliers.

I got onto an incredible journey of learning and, perhaps empowerment in a way, where I was delivering a £30,000,000 project. That came out of nowhere and became one of the strongest strategic priorities of the Council at the time to try and address this digital challenge.

All of that was driven by a question from an IT manager at the time and him giving me the freedom and the flexibility to go and address that and then to make it happen. So, a lot of thanks to him and I think it's around that memory of being able to just take that on and try something as adventurous as that in the public sector which was quite new at the time.

Who was the best boss you ever had and why?

It was a the IT manager at the County Council because he gave me the freedom to grow and develop.

What was the greatest challenge you faced as a middle manager?

Sometimes it's about navigating your way through to perhaps where you want to be and understanding how to get there.

Some of those ways through in career development aren't always as straight forward and linear. Quite often you might have to take a step sideward to go up rather than a direct path through.

Linked to that, I have experienced, as many others have, people and things which are barriers to that growth. Things can hold you back and it's understanding how to deal with that and find a way either around it or to work with it to achieve where you want to get.

I have got some examples in my career where there have been people that have not necessarily wanted me to succeed. Or rather, my ambition hasn't been matched with their ambitions, sometimes I've seen that as a threat. So, perhaps working with that and understanding that, and understanding their viewpoint becomes increasingly more important the more senior you get.

I would suggest over the years, understanding people and their emotions is key. Emotional intelligence is a key part in trying to understand how you work against those challenges and look for those advocates in a business that can help you with that as well. So, it's been very helpful to have several senior sponsors, champions, or people that you might call mentors, to help me.

I remember a job previously that was in the private sector. I've always been ambitious so I always had an aspiration to advance my career and being quite assertive to move things forward. This was reflected back to me by a manager at the time. He said: 'Are you aware it's an almost selfish level of ambition that you have and that's not impacting as well as it could do onto your team and the workforce?'

And that was a step back moment. I realised I needed to do things slightly differently. I needed to work with people in a different way. I had to understand how my actions and my interactions with other people can get the best out of a situation, get the best out of them and the best for me. So I quickly started to consciously learn more about the emotional intelligence side of things. I wouldn't say I am an expert, everybody has their blind spots, but that's been an important part of my learning journey and development. I've gone through management and understood how to work with people in that way.

What was the biggest mistake you made when you were a middle manager?

I know this sort of sounds rather clichéd, but I don't tend to look back at mistakes in a negative way. I don't think that's the right or helpful way to do things. I think you might want to learn from mistakes, but I've always seen those as constructive opportunities to do so. I am very much a glass half full person. Very optimistic. I see things very positively and if there has been a mistake, I've probably seen that as an opportunity for learning either for myself or helping others learn.

Perhaps on occasions where there has been a mistake, I am more mindful of if it, if I've let other people down. But I think the moves I've made in my career, decisions I've made, I've always done based on best possible information and intelligence at that time.

I think probably if I had to reflect what was my biggest area of learning where mistakes may have originated from it was that eagerness to please. Not saying no to things.

I was guilty of taking on more responsibility and pressure. Other people recognised that characteristic in me and took advantage of it a little bit. I wouldn't say it was a mistake as such, but I now know that it's a tendency of mine. There are only so many hours in a day and I can't be superhuman, and there are limits and it does impact a lot on other facets of your life.

So at one point it did feel like I was nearly doing about three people's jobs.

I did just get on with it but, in hindsight, that probably wasn't necessary, it was around me trying to prove myself and get on the next rung of the ladder.

So, that's probably my area of weaknesses, taking too much on. And sometimes not necessary delegating enough of that as well.

What personal qualities do you see in the best middle managers?

Passion. **Drive**. A willingness to move things forward. I would rephrase that in terms of **positivity**. They're well organised, they've got a clear direction of where they want to be which is helpful.

They have a plan how to get there. Whether it's right or wrong. But they are quietly confident in what they do.

I would suggest the perhaps more overt kind of person that is willing to push their way through, doesn't come across as a leader to me. That comes out as somebody wanting career progression rather than someone that can get the best out of his colleagues and his team.

That's really what I would look for in a leader. So, they get the job done and they support the rest of the organisation as well as potentially having a set of technical skills that can take them to a particular place.

I also look for qualities and skills that are different to mine because if you had company full of me, I don't think it would be a very good company at all.

What skills do you think middle managers should focus on developing to ensure their effectiveness over their career?

I am convinced that many people will have more of a portfolio career. What I mean by that is that a person won't be in a job for a long period of time and they may not even work in the same organisation for a long period of time.

And that seems to become more commonplace. So, really, what we're looking for in the next 10 to 15 years will be people that have good resilience, and adaptability to new environments and new situations. The ability to communicate well and get on with people in different and challenging circumstances. As well as understanding change management and how to implement change effectively. And the willingness to work on shorter time cycles for delivery of whatever the project is. I also think there is value in having a variety of skills and experience from different sectors and perspectives.

This will become increasingly important compared to 10 or 20 years ago.

This was reinforced by a conversation I had with somebody from the creative and digital industry recently. They were saying in their industry they have operated in a career portfolio manner for several years. People take small jobs and move from one job to the next and to the next. People are becoming increasingly entrepreneurial and moving from one contract to the other. I think that's going to be really important in the long term for leadership skills that people have strong emotional intelligence as well as the intellectual intelligence to really get the best out of people in different environments.

What do you know now that you wish you knew as a middle manager?

That it's not a race. I had an aspiration to be a director by the time I was 40. I achieved that one when I was probably 36 so ahead of my schedule, and I was quite pleased with myself for doing that.

But it doesn't need to be a race to chase the money and to chase a position. I think it's more important to build up the skills and capabilities as you go.

Doing something once and moving it on, doesn't mean you can put it on your CV that you've done it. You've really got to have to build a depth of experience in certain areas. And that comes over time.

When I say not being a race, clearly you want to try and get there as quickly as you can but don't do that at the expense of forfeiting your skills and capabilities as you are moving on.

Practice it, not just once but twice, three times and build your capabilities. Otherwise you can find as you get further up the ladder, unless you feel like you have the experts beneath you, you may not think you know it as well as you could do.

I also think building a network early is key.

As is constantly learning and developing yourself and becoming educated and good at what you do.

What's your one Tip for the Top?

It would be have somebody in either the sector or in a senior role that can be your mentor.

Somebody that can actually help and guide you. Someone that a short conversation with might be able to actually solve half a day's worth of consideration. Not someone to do the job for you, but somebody that you can actually work with to bounce ideas that off that has been there and done it.

During different parts of my career I've had those opportunities. As I think back to those people they have helped me make different decisions. Because as a middle manager, typically your exposure to a person at the top is where you're taking a decision to or a briefing or a report. It's a very linear relationship.

Whereas having somebody who isn't connected in that way means you can have a different style of conversation. They see things from a different perspective and might be able to suggest areas, blind spots, development opportunities and strengths to you that you may not see yourself. Or he or she may be able to help you enhance those in a different way.

So, it would be to have that confidante or a mentor from somebody at the top.

What is the one book you'd recommend to every middle manager?

This is quite sad actually; it was when I was a middle manager aspiring to become a senior leader. I remember reading a book on holiday sadly, but somewhere where nobody could see.

It was the Seven Habits of Highly Effective People by Stephen Covey.

What question haven't I asked that you think I should have?

I suppose, it's a crowded market moving to the top. There's lots of people that aspire to be at the top. There are limited posts to do that, so it would be potentially of asking a middle manager: 'Why do they want to be at the top'?

Asking a middle manager to appreciate and really understand why they want to be at the top, might help them make better decisions on how to get there in a certain way. Also being aware of what timescale they have in mind, because being at the top could mean something very different to different people. Let's just use an example.

Somebody says: 'I want to be a Managing Director'. You can quit your job now you can go and create your own business and overnight you're a Managing Director is that what you want? "Oh no, I want the salary to go with it". I think it's just really understanding why they want to get there and where do they want to get to.

What two things have struck you most from what was said?

What one thing will you do differently/employ as a result of what you've learnt from this chapter?

14

Katrina Michelle

Chief Executive, Marketing Cheshire

Katrina's career has been spent largely working in multinational communications agencies, but she's topped and tailed it with two slightly different things. When she left university, she went into the Foreign Office, where she worked for five years as a junior diplomat. In the last five years Katrina has been Chief Executive of Marketing Cheshire. Marketing Cheshire is a destination management organisation, which deals with generating tourism and inward investment.

What was your best memory or achievement as a middle manager?

That's quite easy because, in about 1990–'91, I was luckily enough to work with the team at Publicis in London, who were tasked with launching the Renault Clio in the UK. After a few false starts we developed the Nicole and Papa idea. Now, initially the idea was a lot broader than just two people in the car. It was a whole world of funny French characters. But, in the end we narrowed it down to Nicole and her dad, who both found that the Clio suited them for their lifestyle. That campaign, when it finally ran, doubled

Renault's market share in the UK from 3% to 6% within a couple of years. This really scared the likes of Ford and Vauxhall. That was definitely one of those times when the stars really collided, and it was a real team effort in persuading both the UK and French clients that having this slightly sexy, you know older/younger dynamic was going to work for the car, but it did.

Who was the best boss you ever had and why?

That's easy as well. I've worked with lots of really good people. I've worked for Martin Sorrell in the past and some of his senior managers. Obviously, I've worked for various ambassadors when I was at the Foreign Office. However, the best boss is a guy called David Bell, who had an agency in Manchester called Cheetham Bell, which was bought by J. Walter Thompson in about about 2000, I think.

Dave is the best boss I had because he could do your job better than you ever could, but let you get on with it. But, when you got stuck, Dave went home and came back with an answer. I mean he was a great example of leadership by example. I don't think he was great at the minutiae and micromanagement, but he was very good at the vision thing and creating an ethos for the team that everybody wanted to buy into. He was very successful both creatively and in business for quite some time. But now I think he works on his own as a consultant and still is a hugely creative person. So, he's my number one.

What was the greatest challenge you faced as a middle manager?

There were some really basic challenges, you know. It is quite hard to juggle two kids and a job and all that sort of thing, but it's not impossible. So, I wouldn't say it's the greatest challenge. Women have been doing that since God was in short trousers. But there is a period in the middle of your career when there's a number of things that you need to be dealing with if you want to keep going. So, that, and I'm not saying that I'm really different from anybody else, but you know the perception of you at that stage is you're not firing on all cylinders.

Another challenge is to know there's a certain point when people just perceptually think you're past it. But, there's also a perception that once you're with a couple of kids that you're not going to be quite on the button all time, so you have to deal with that. You have to deal with it in a nice way with a smile on your face.

The other challenge I had to deal with is when I moved out of London. I'd been going along on my happy way, zooming up the ladder in various big advertising agencies. Then in 1998 my career changed a lot when I was going happily along in one trajectory, and all of a sudden for various reasons I moved out of London and moved to Manchester.

I had to adapt to a completely different set of clients, competitive situations, people with different skill sets and sometimes better skill sets because they could do a lot more. But also, the fact that business was a lot harder to come by. It just didn't drop in your lap in the way it does in London. And culturally it took a while to get my head round that. We made a great success of it. I always actually think it was easier to work in London. There was just more to go at. You had to really ... what's the right word ... sort of tease it out up north.

What was the biggest mistake you made when you were a middle manager?

I think it's a mistake many people make and that is opportunities are put in front of you, and you think you're not ready.

I had an opportunity to become number two at quite a big agency, and it was a more general manager job and not my main skill set. I've had an MBA from INSEAD, so I should have been completely arrogant and thought I could do everything. But, at that stage I thought, "Oh, my God, can I do it? Am I ready? Am I ready?"

I didn't take it and I should have done it. So, that was a big mistake, to let my fear and self-doubt get in the way. Life would have been very different if I'd done that. It may have all ended in tears, but I think I would have repositioned myself in the light of everybody else as a senior manager, rather than as sort of a head of a function, which is what I was.

That role would have put me into the senior management team.

What personal qualities do you see in the best middle managers?

Well, I suppose I'm a bit naughty really, because I'm not too bothered about what's in someone's CV. I wasn't great academically, and I've got quite a good CV. Nowadays I wouldn't pass the screening of most computers. You know my grades at A level are probably not quite high enough and my degree is a 2.2, so that probably wouldn't get through the screening process.

So, I tend to take the view that what I'm looking for is **motivation**, an **engaging personality**, the **ability to get on with people**. Because the business I work in people is a people business, and if people don't like you they're not going to buy from you basically. I tend to also look for someone who is willing to have a go at anything.

So, that's not very good, because sometimes you do need someone with a lot of technical competence. But, I kind of think you can learn it. I think you can learn most things if you want to enough. But, what you can't learn is the ability to form rapport with clients.

In a communications business, that's not good, no matter how smart they were. As an example, I had someone who had been head boy at his school and thought the world owed him a living. I got him headhunted out, because the clients were just saying, "He's an arrogant bastard, and we don't like him." That was going to cost me money eventually. So, I tend to quickly scan the CV and once we've gone through that, I'm really just looking for somebody who I think has got the right attitude. If they've obviously proved to be unbelievably incompetent, then I've just got that one down to experience. But on the whole, attitude counts more than ability generally in my book.

What skills do you think middle managers should focus on developing to ensure their effectiveness over their career?

Finance, because obviously a lot of senior managers, board directors or chief execs and chairmen are accountants. There's a reason for that. It's not necessarily something we all want to admit to, but at the end of the day companies go bust if you don't understand the various ratios and numbers and warning signs that your management information is giving you.

Obviously in small companies this is incredibly important, but you know we've seen examples recently. There was a business in Crewe, where there was a £30million discrepancy in the accounts. The chief exec at the time, apparently used to like sitting in her Range Rover and commanding and controlling on her hands-free phone. But she managed to miss a £30million hole in her own accounts. Seriously, dear, where were you?

So, finance, even if it's not your strong suit, there are some real basics that you need to understand. That way you can mix it in the board room, and I've been a non-executive director for quite a few companies. You just don't come across well if in five minutes you can't say something intelligent about the accounts. So, start there.

Then I think the other thing is having a strong network. Know everyone. Get to know people, even if you just basically know them on a hello basis. Because when it comes to thinking about who's going to run the company, they'll know you.

Get to know everybody. Get to know everybody in your company. Get to know everybody in your sector. Make sure that you know what's going on in your city. Get to know how the public sector works. Get to know a few people in each network, and not just the same network. Lots of people turn up for the chamber of commerce and think that's it.

What do you know now that you wish you knew as a middle manager?

One thing that has kind of dawned on me now in my later years, is that that the way that the public sector manages people is really quite different from the way that people's careers develop in the private sector. I don't want to make a value judgement about one is better than the other, but it does produce very different results, I think.

You notice in the private sector that people tend to move on and get different experiences, diversify their experience a bit, and maybe eventually come to something that they are good at. But experience can be transferred across from different things, so that makes you sort of hopefully better and a rounder manager.

What I find in the public sector though is that the rewards and recognition are quite different and not necessarily analogous with what you get rewarded for in the private sector. I think it is a bit of a problem, and it's almost a societal problem. This lack of an injection of different thinking across the two sectors, has led a stifled and sometimes inefficient public sector.

I think if I'd had my career again, I would have liked to have jumped across a bit at the beginning, so a bit of public, bit of private, took the best of both. Then basically used that in my career. I think that should be massively encouraged, so that you take the best of everything. I don't like the public/private divide, I think we should try and encourage a lot more symbiosis.

I know government for example is going to hire dozens of people in to manage Brexit. But culturally, are they ready for it?

What's your one Tip for the Top?

Be nice to people, and never shut a door too hard basically. I don't like the Donald Trump style of management. That's why I think if you do shut the door too hard, if you are nasty to people, cut off relationships with people, you are precluding potential future relationships. After I left Cheetham Bell

JWT, I set up a consultancy with a friend of mine , which we ran for three years successfully.

My first contract, which was a big contract, came from somebody I hadn't worked with for 20 years. But I was able to pick up the phone and say, "Hi, how are you? What're you doing?" They said, "Oh, what are you doing?" I told them what I was doing and they replied, "Oh, thank God for that, because I've got this client and I don't have a clue what to do. Can you come and help me?" I literally hadn't worked with them for 20 years.

That was never shut the door too hard basically. I have shut the door hard, and it's really come back to bite me.

What is the one book you'd recommend to every middle manager?

I'm going to cheat a bit here. I think a boxed set of Mad Men might not be a bad thing to do.

Because I think over the course of Mad Men we see every trick in the book. The combination of Don Draper and his pitching techniques and Roger Sterling and his client service and his slightly dirty dealings, and the way that Joan tries to get herself up the corporate ladder. I mean it's all in there.

So, rather than pick one management guru, who all have their moment in the sun, and they all make one key point.

What question haven't I asked that you think I should have?

Why aren't I earning more than I am?

Well, the answer is because life has to be full of challenges and difference isn't it?

I was working in London for Ogilvy and Mather on American Express and Unilever, big global brands, learning a lot of stuff about Chinese consumers. It was really, really interesting. I was earning a lot of money. Then a local job came up and it was about making a bit of a difference locally, or at least kind of understanding why we're not making a big difference locally. It was massively underfunded, I had to go out and scrabble for money. But it introduced me to loads of people.

Sometimes, interesting jobs don't come with big pay packets. So, maybe the thing to say to middle managers, if you're not enjoying what you're doing, find out if you could maybe do a job that you would like doing and suck up the fact that the money might have to go down for a bit before it goes up again.

I think the French say, 'Reculer pour mieux sauter,' which means pull back to jump better. So, it's not a bad thing to do.

Sometimes you have to just take your balls in both hands and say, "Do you know what? This could be fun." And, it has been fun. Very exhausting, sometimes usually frustrating, but actually my life is much more enriched. Would it have been much more enriched by another five years working on American Express and Unilever? Maybe not.

What two things have struck you most from what was said?

What one thing will you do differently/employ as a result of what you've learnt from this chapter?

15

Ken Perry

Founder and Director of Do-Well (UK) Ltd

Ken founded Do-Well, a leadership practice in 2014. Prior to that he was Chief Executive for 14 years at Plus Dane Housing, a large social housing landlord in the North West. During his time there the business grew from an organisation that employed about 200 people with a turnover over £13 million to 1,000 people and a turnover of £100 million. He was just 35 when he took over as CEO and the youngest of any housing association in the UK at the time.

What would be your best achievement when you were in that middle management sphere?

It depends how you judge "best". I've got a competitive streak that is interesting, because I'm generally not competitive for myself but I tend to be competitive for others. There has been a number of times where the organisation that I led was in competition with much larger organisations and nobody had expected my organisation to win the work or grow. On each occasion we did. So, I think from a competitive point of view, there are things that I'm proud of.

Most of all, though, I'm proud of the things that the organisation did. There were people who worked with me who are doing things now they never dreamt possible. There were residents and tenants that we worked for who went to places, achieved things, and started businesses.

Going back to my first answer, the things I'm most proud of is the success I've enabled in other people. I think commercially, obviously, the organisation grew and flourished and did more and different things and that was important, but that wasn't the end; it was a means to an end.

In a traditional commercial sense, if you improve the profitability, the scale and the turnover of the organisation, that's the point. But in the work that I've done, serving my time as a Chief Exec, that was the beginning. It's a bit like conversations around mergers and acquisitions, I always feel very strongly that they aren't strategies in themselves, but some people forget that.

For me, in summary, I would be lying if I didn't say some highlights were successful business and competition things. That's true. But mainly because it led us to do more things, to serve more people.

When I left my old job, somebody wrote to me and said: "If it hadn't been for my work with you, I would be dead". Not only had he started working and had bought his own house, but both of his sons had started working, and his grandson. They were lives transformed, not by me, but by things that I'd enabled to happen. That reminded me that I had done some decent work.

When you were rising up the ranks, though, before you got to Chief Executive, what was your favourite achievement or memory from that period?

In the early 1990's I went through a long and extensive competitive process for a middle manager's job. So much so, I think my mum thought I was applying to be the Prime Minister. In the end my application was successful however on my first day when I turned up, the Director that had recruited me had forgotten and had put nothing in place to welcome and induct me into the organisation.

This new role was still a middle manager's job, but it was a big step up for me. The brief was to establish a completely new service. I had a choice then, I could have stepped back and thought, "I need to wait for the senior management to give me my brief." Or the other option, the one that I took, was to say to myself, "okay, well, I'm quite a resilient person. I'll go and find the people who are doing this work at the moment, sit with them, find out what's necessary, and just get started."

I didn't know anybody, and I didn't know the area. I didn't know who was going to be supportive. There was a political dimension to what we were doing as well.

Within two years, we made the new service happen. This involved establishing a whole new office, bringing a whole bunch of people together who'd not worked together before and also involving people who were outside of the organisation as well.

In many ways, life is a bit like that from a resilience point of view. You can either accept your lot or you can say, "What can I take from this?" and that's a good example of me doing that.

Looking back over your career, who has been the best boss you've ever had and why?

That's an interesting one, because I recently had the opportunity to tell that person. They've just retired so we went for a drink together and I was able to tell him and say 'thank you.'

The reason that he was the best boss that I've had was because he took a risk on me. That, interestingly, links to the previous story, because I moved into this role after a short stay in the other organisation and it was a sideways move for me. I went partly because I liked what that company was doing. I liked the fact that he went out of his way to encourage me to accept the job, he even brought the contract of employment to my flat where I was living at the time.

But the main reason is he had confidence in me. He gave me a clear idea of what was required and then let me get on with it and that's confidence.

He was confident enough in his own ability to recognise that he had super people in lots of different positions. I think that's not something that everyone feels confident enough to do. I've always tried to follow that route and say that you don't make yourself look tall by surrounding yourself with small people. I've seen him do really well using that approach and he's retired well as a consequence.

What was the greatest challenge you faced when you were in that middle management position?

I experienced a common challenge that faces most people when they move into their first or second manager's job.

In circumstances where you've come from a position of professional competence or technical knowledge, if there's a gap in your team, it's very easy to fall into the trap of filling it yourself, which isn't good practice at all but most people do it.

Once you learn that it's not best practice, you find yourself in a position where you can't step into a gap that's left by someone else.

113

I think that's a key learning point. You need to know the skills that your broader responsibility takes on board, and plan for that. Things like having good succession planning and thinking about the risk of key people leaving.

You don't fully realise this until you live that experience. I often still work with people who think, "well, I could turn my hand to anything in this business." Even if that's true, the chances are the world has moved on quite significantly since you did it.

Equally, even when you're a first line manager and you're managing people who do the work you used to, there is a temptation to think your way is the only way.

Then you get focused on managing process not outcome. There's some hard learning in all of this. The important thing is making sure that you are leading and managing both and recognising that, when you move up to that next level, where there are people who are doing work you can't do. So make sure that you have a proper plan for if and when they leave, either positively or not.

What personal qualities do you see in the best middle managers?

I think middle management is under threat as a whole concept. Traditionally, middle managers have been the people who have given permission for things, held onto information, distributed resources and communicated things. That is a tough job in lots of ways because you're in the middle of everything.

I think the middle generally is threatened in every level in society because access to information is pretty much available to everybody. All levels in an organisation are sighted on things like business plan content, performance information and financial information and increasingly, the generation that are coming through don't want to be bossed and directed; they want to find their own way. The traditional roles of a middle manager around control and co-ordination are changing.

I think it's a timely question, because middle management is probably subject of another book. It needs to be rethought.

Some of the things that are important are recognising you can't do everything yourself. I think there's a real temptation in middle managers to think, "I'd show them how to do it, but it's easier to do it myself."

It's a classic mistake that most fall into, especially under pressure. I've done it as well. I think the best middle managers are the ones who are able to translate the complexity of what's going on in the organisation and the world, maybe, and turn that into very clear asks of the people that they work with. I suspect that skill, and the need for that skill, will continue, but I think the supervision element that has been valued more highly is less required now.

Similarly, the argument of whether people can work at home or need to work in an office is a debate that's still raging. One of the biggest barriers is the question of how do we know people are working if they're at home, even though there are lots of ways you can measure that. By outcome, through technology, and other things.

That's been a traditional middle manager role: have people come in on time, have they left on time? And in some cases, that's necessary. But I suppose my argument is, it's increasingly less so. Because it's self-evident. People know whether they've done the work.

A good example would be in appraisal. At middle manager level, where sometimes you don't really need your boss to tell you that you've done something wrong. Probably most people will know that. The trick is what you do with the error.

I think the best middle managers are the ones who say, "Okay that didn't go so well. What have we learned?". That of course then makes people much more comfortable coming forward when they have made a mistake.

The worst middle managers are the ones who try and rule by fear but of course, that's not sustainable, and things are hidden from them.

So I would say, the best middle managers are the ones, certainly for the future, that are able to **understand complexity**, **articulate that clearly**, **guide people**, and **coach** and **mentor** them going forward. I think that'll be a new generation of skills that will be required for middle managers.

In terms of the qualities that perhaps support those skills, what would you say they are for you?

I think a middle manager is in the same as managers at any level. You're looking for a high degree of authenticity and transparency. In some organisations that Do-Well is working with on cultural development or organisational development, or change, we are seeing people who are in middle manager roles and feel they have to be something else other than themselves.

People talk about putting a particular face on, whatever it might be. My challenge to people is to ask 'why?' Because ultimately people will commit to people if they share their values and they understand why they're doing what they're doing. I think often we don't bring enough of ourselves to the workplace. The best middle managers are people who can operate in a way that means people will commit to the work that they're asking them to do. They resort to forced compliance as little as possible.

Obviously, there are certain things that things have to be done, but if you're a good middle manager, you'll know that and I think that overlaps with some of the things I talked about earlier in terms of how times are changing. The days of the overseer, supervisor, those sorts of things have got to go, for competitive organisations anyway.

What do you know now that you wish you knew back then, when you were in middle management?

Pace yourself, probably, and don't take yourself too seriously.

I think sometimes, especially when you're young for senior positions you can lose perspective. I can remember in one of my very first manager's jobs and the long hours that I put in, because it was so important. I put myself under so much pressure.

I couldn't tell you now what I was doing. I used to say that if I was my own boss, I'd take a grievance out against myself because I was always too unreasonable. I think a lot of people can do that and your expectation of others can be different as well.

I think probably I would say to myself, "don't work so long. Don't be too hard on yourself. And remember that things take time. Long-term change takes time. It's not all about you in that sense."

As a younger person, and younger manager, I think you can take yourself way too seriously and that doesn't necessarily make you the best version of yourself. I would tell myself to think about why I was doing the work I was doing, and what my drivers were. I think everything was very frantic for reasons, now that I couldn't tell you.

Also, be clear about the difference between what work you are doing and what your job is and recognise that there's a difference between the two. That makes you quite resilient, knowing the difference between the two things.

What would be your one tip for the top?

Definitely, without any shadow of a doubt, it is to be really, really clear why you're doing the work that you're doing.

In all of my experience of people that do well, it's the people who want the work, not the job. I've sat on this side of the desk for many interviews of senior people, Directors, Chief Execs, Chairs of organisations. The people who don't succeed are the ones who want the job. They want to be a Director of anywhere, a Chief Executive of anywhere. They want the role and that's very unattractive.

I think that's where, sadly, some of the hero leadership type texts and programs like The Apprentice and all of those things, give people a wrong-headed view of what ambition is.

It's much more attractive to be ambitious for a higher cause and people are much more likely to work with you and help you and assist you with your work.

The people who are successful, and the ones who are successful in the longer run, want to do the work. They want to do whatever the work of the business might be, end poverty, house people, solve inequality, deal with health inequalities. If that's their work, and they articulate that well, the job's gone.

And what would be one book that you would recommend every middle manager read?

That's a great question.

I read a book just before I started Do-Well, called "Consiglieri: Leading from the Shadows." It's a book about being a number two in an organisation. Consiglieri, as you probably know, is a mafia model. The godfather has a Consiglieri, who is their number two and isn't family. So that person can never be number one, because they're not family. That's where the name comes from.

The author of the book was a Deputy Chairman for one of the main marketing companies, I think Saatchi and Saatchi. He spoke at an event I went to and what he was saying was: "We don't really talk enough about what a wonderful role it is being a deputy to somebody. Because chances are, you're on the board. Almost certainly you will have influence on that board and outside. You'll have the ear of the chair, the ear of the Chief Executive. And you have an ability to get things done. But the ultimate responsibility doesn't sit with you. And you'll be very well rewarded."

The whole issue with the book, I think, is interesting, because we have this sort of drive within us of ways to think, "I need to be number one." If someone said someone is a really good number two, people then translate that to think that they are not quite good enough to be number one. The whole book is a celebration of thinking about where your skills are best used.

I know from 14 years lived experience that being that number one has got lots of things that are great about it, but the thing that tires you in the end, is that it is lonely.

It's just you.

I'd recommend it, because it might make people think about what it is they're trying to achieve. You don't have to be the top person in an organisation to be successful. I think to be successful you need to be doing the right work with the right people. And that's where happiness, fulfilment, and your own success comes from.

Where we become unhappy is where that ends, one way or another, we find ourselves working in places and for people who we don't align with and no matter how much money you get, it doesn't compensate you for that.

It can happen drip by drip. And then one day you wake up and you think, "How am I here? How did that happen?" The key thing is knowing it, and then doing something about it.

I think "Consiglieri: Leading from the Shadows" is a good book to read for a couple of reasons.

One is it might make you refocus what your own ambition is. Secondly, it makes you realise that actually you can achieve a lot and be successful if you choose deliberately not to be the Chief Exec or the Chair of an organisation.

One of the things I realised more than anything else is I quite like influence. I don't have to be the person who makes the big speech or writes the report or whatever it might be. What's more important is that that speech or that report makes a difference, a positive difference, in one way or another. That's more important. And that feels more sustainable, I think, in the long run.

What question haven't I asked you that you think I might have?

I suppose considering our shared interest in resilience: "How do you keep going?"

One of the things that I recognise is that the people who do well are the ones who just keep going.

This links to my message to my younger self about self-care. To spend time looking after yourself is not self-indulgent. It's vital. You wouldn't buy a high-end sports car and not put any petrol in it, or not maintain it.

So I think making sure you eat properly and make sure you take time to do the five ways to wellbeing. When I was a younger manager, it felt a bit self-indulgent, but it's really not. Recognising that you cannot lead and serve other people well if you are exhausted, burnt out, and stressed out is really important. Like most people, I had to feel that before I did anything about it.

People will come to that conclusion but unless they've actually felt that pain, sometimes they don't change. I think in that sense, I probably would have thought we'd have had a question about that and that would have been my answer. But I know it's not easy for people, but it's very, very important.

What two things have struck you most from what was said?

What one thing will you do differently/employ as a result of what you've learnt from this chapter?

16

Lee Collins

Founder & CEO, Revilo Group

Lee Collins had a group of car companies that he sold in 2014. He sold those companies, and then technically retired...for 69 days.

Lee then started a company called Revilo Capital. Revilo Capital owns a lot of residential and commercial property. Because Lee was interested in business in general, he found a model where he invests in individuals and creates businesses around them, which means they have created six new companies in the last three years, all from scratch. The businesses include: new startup investment, residential & commercial landlord, property developers, new house builders, automotive specialists, business consultants, estate agents, insurance specialists and mortgages brokers. They are all based in Rochdale.

What was your best memory or achievement as a middle manager?

I started off on a YTS on £25 pounds a week then left school at 16. I got a work placement at a plastics factory and worked there for a few years. And then the plastics factory got a government grant so that they effectively paid for them to build a new factory in an underprivileged area. This turned out to be London, so they took the government's money and then shut their old factory down. So, for all the jobs they created, they made everybody else redundant, so it was just one of these stupid scenarios.

I always had a passion for cars so, I started off selling cars for Lookers in Rochdale. My parents thought I was crazy. Then as I got some experience and I took on different management roles. I was very fortunate that I was good at what I did, so my career accelerated at a quick pace. But then eventually, you get to the point where you're running the company, so you're responsible for everything. And then, what's left to do? Really, I was making somebody else very wealthy even though they were paying me very well. So, I was running a group of companies on behalf of the people who owned it then when I was 30.

Eventually, I realised that the bottom line is that you're going to have to do it for yourself. So, I think going back to the start of the question, the biggest issue is raising funding to be able to make that transition. And I think it's at least if not more challenging today than it was back in the day. At the time, I sold my house and everything we had and went into a rented house and put it all on the line and borrowed the rest from the bank. Today, it would be at least as difficult but probably more difficult to do the same thing.

Who was the best boss you ever had and why?

I'm still friends with him. We probably go out for dinner twice a year. He gave me my first senior role in management. And it was an interesting role, because he was painful. I think if you talk to my most of my team, they would say I'm painful about getting it right and what we expect and so on and so forth. But he was 10 times worse than me.

I worked with him for three years, and even now, that's some 20 odd years ago, it still feels in my mind that that was the place I worked the longest, which is not the case. I only worked there for three years, but in my mind, it felt like I was there for 20 years.

I think the reason for that is because that was the time when I learned so much. So as much as he spent most of his life stood on me and pulling my arms off, whilst he was doing that he was educating me as to why I was in that predicament in the first place. That was an influential time in my life and why I will always hold him on a bit of a pedestal even though it was a stressful time and it wasn't very enjoyable, or so it felt at the time.

He unfortunately had a business that went bust several years later, which was through no fault of his own. It was a large supplier that went bust and effectively took them with them, which is often the case. The day I found out, I went around and I took my car and I left my car with him because he basically lost everything, and said, "Just keep the car until you're back on your feet." We were fortunate to have more than one car.

That was the regard that I had for him even though back then we hadn't worked together for maybe 15 years or something. But because I will always view him as being responsible for a large lift in my career getting me where I wanted to go, I'll always have this regard for him even though he was very painful to work for.

So, I think there's a moral in that, isn't there? The fact that the guy or the lady that you're working with that's going to do you the best is not necessarily the easiest to work with.

And I think a lot of people miss that.

If you work with somebody who's just dead nice and everything is great and they're pleased with every single thing you do, you got to ask yourself how much you're actually learning on this journey? It's easy to end up doing a bit of daydreaming about this, that, and the other. If you were daydreaming for three and a half seconds with Richard, he found something that was wrong with something you should have been managing across the company.

He was the most informed man, I think, I've ever met, and it was like he had a crystal ball and he just knew what was happening. So, he would ask you a question and you just knew that was the only question you didn't know the answer to. The other 999 answers you had like that, but he would ask you the one thing that you didn't know, and then he would vilify you for not knowing.

What was the biggest mistake you made when you were a middle manager?

It's difficult to say I've not made a big mistake, but one thing comes to mind.

I have a friend who manufactures soft drinks, and we were sat in our office having a coffee one day and at the time his business had turned over that year £50 million , and our business had turned over £55 million. He made £14 million profit and we made a £1 million. So, we had a bigger business and we were making a fraction of what he was making. The difference was not the way we operated. It was just the fact that there's more money in soft drinks than there were in other products.

So, I think given the chance to do it all over again, maybe a sector of the market that was more profitable might have been an interesting way to go. But without being crass, I'm a self-made multimillionaire, so what have I got to complain about? It really is what it is.

I think if I did it all over again, I might have tried to do certain things quicker in my career even though my career was well advanced at a pretty young age. I bought the business from the original owners in 2006. So, I'd been with the company then for nine years. So, if anything, that nine years, in a perfect world, I would've liked to have been less.

What personal qualities do you see in the best middle managers?

To me, there are key things. It's what we looked for back in the day, and it's what we look for today, and I can't imagine it ever changing. Every single person we speak to, if we're looking either to make an investment or we're looking at offering them employment or whatever, the thing that stands out for me head and shoulders is attitude.

So, when we look at CVs, it's great to see people with degrees and it's great to see people with 12 GCSEs and so on and so forth. But if you come in here for a conversation and you've got a poor attitude to either the discussion, life, the way the world treats you, I probably can't help you. Most of the things we do in business we can teach people, but I can't give you common sense and I can't give you a good attitude if you've got a bad one. And if you've got a bad attitude, I can work with you and I can bring about what is typically a temporary change, and that might work for a week, it might work for a month, it might work for six months, but eventually, you'll go back to where you naturally sit. And that's a problem in business for me.

So, my eldest son is 19, and he's done his GCSEs. He's done his A-levels and he's working within the business now as opposed to going to university, but he might go after 12 months out. But the one thing he gets stopped in his tracks for any single hour of any day is if his attitude is short on what we'd expect it to be. And it will be the same for all of them.

My view on work and people's attitude is different from most. I'm really quite pedantic about the small things that we do. In a past life where we had a beverage area for customers, we had to have nine coffee cups. We didn't have ten, and you couldn't have eight. Now, people would often say to me, "Why are you so anally retentive about nine cups?"

And I'd reply, "Well, because you've got to get into the psyche of the people. If they understand that eight is no good and ten is no good and you're going to make an issue out of how many coffee cups there are, imagine what they're thinking when they're talking to your customers, when they're walking around the building, when they get dressed in the morning and whether they clean their shoes and so on and so forth."

I want them to think, 'The man at the top, he's crazy about how many coffee cups we've got. Well, you can bet your bottom dollar he's crazy about how you're talking to your customers, how you're doing what you're paid to do and if we are doing what we said we were going to do?'

So, the little things in life and making a focus around them can have a tremendous effect on the way people work in general. If you have a bad attitude, you're never, ever going to get that. If you think, "It's just coffee cups." Well, it's not.

Boeing don't have 20 different ways of attaching an aircraft wing to a fuselage. They have one way of doing it. If they get it wrong, wings fall off and people die. Because the risks are less in lots of other commercial operations, people have a different view. They just think, "Well, if it's worth doing, how come there is not the right way and a right process for doing things?"

There has to be one that's more efficient, and there has to be one that has normally a better outcome. So, if we standardise that and make sure that that happens all the time, we have a more successful business.

So, attitude is not just about whether you're nice and polite and all the rest of it. It feeds into your entire contribution and how successful we will be as a business.

What skills do you think middle managers should focus on developing to ensure their effectiveness over their career?

I think, it's an obvious one to say it now, but it still surprises me how many IT illiterate people there are. You don't need to be an IT expert to work in most workplaces, unless, of course, that's your job. But it never ceases to amaze me how many people have huge difficulty using Microsoft Excel or struggling to send an email or they have a problem with something and it should be relatively easy to fix and the whole world comes crashing down.

I obviously grew up in a time when there was no internet and we didn't all have personal computers. So, I think it was about '94 when as a business the only people in the business that had computers were the accounts department, everything was running on MS-DOS based systems at the time. I just had this kind of inkling that it was going to become such a bigger thing. I don't really know why. I'd love to make some claim of being able to see into the future. But it was just that kind of thought that everybody is going to end up using them.

So, I went out and spent my own money at Currys, and I think it was £1800 pounds at the time, which in '94 was a lot of money. It would've been a machine that had no power whatsoever and you were using a 56K-dial up modem. I got this machine home and struggled like you do, or you did back in the day trying to get my head around how everything worked. It seems stupid now, but even the plugs on the back of desktops were all colour coded for your mouse, keyboard and everything else, so that there were idiot proof in a way.

And then I just spent every bit of spare time I had messing about with a computer. Of course, as time went on that became a much bigger thing, but when I sit here today, and I'm a big fan of technology, my knowledge of technology is pretty good.

The one thing that I find really surprising today is that there are people coming out of school and so on and so forth with very, very little knowledge about how to operate a computer. You say to someone, "This is Microsoft Excel. Do you know how it works?" and they look at you like you're trying to get them to learn Latin.

What do you know now that you wish you knew as a middle manager?

I think that's a really good question. I keep saying to people now that the only advantage I can see of getting older is the fact that there's less new stuff to learn. So pretty much everything that happens I can relate back to a time where I've seen it before, I knew what happened, I knew what fixed it, and I knew what's coming. So, I look at it, and I think actually that's quite a nice place to be, because suddenly I have got to 50, and I feel pretty much in control of everything that's going on in my life. Aside from medical issues or something that you can't foresee, nothing fazes me. Shit happens, and you deal with it accordingly.

I think when I look back, just age and experience is one of those things that there is no shortcut to. I had a chap here the other week and we were doing a mentoring session that he'd requested. He is a young guy and doing very well and earning very well.

He is lacking in patience though. I use the analogy of swimming across a lake. And he was lacking the patience it takes to get from one side to the other. At his age, there was no shortcut because he didn't have the capital to do the things he wanted to do. He didn't have the knowledge to a degree and didn't have the experience. He did have loads of ambition, great attitude, and was doing very well for the age he was at. So, I have no doubt he will do very well in his lifetime, but he was fundamentally beating himself up about not getting where he wanted to go quickly enough instead of recognising where he actually was and how well he was actually doing.

What's your one Tip for the Top?

I talk about this a lot with a lot of people because they come and they want to sit and have a coffee, and sometimes it's our young members of staff and they're young, like a one young lad who is 19, who's working at our estate agency business. One Saturday, I was sat at my desk and he was sat at his, and he kept interjecting about how life had panned out and what I'd done and how I'd manage to achieve that.

My view for getting on in life is just not to expect anything and to go out and make it happen. I think people limit themselves too much as to what they think they can and can't do. And of course, if you think you can or you think you can't, you to prove yourself right, don't you?

I'm always talking to my 19-year-old son and saying, "Look. Nobody has a crystal ball as to what you're going to be doing and what you're going to be successful at when you're my age. So, it doesn't really matter as long as you enjoy the journey. But if you're doing it, do it well. Even if you don't like the job and you're looking for a career change or whatever, have this personal pride that says, 'I'm going to do the very best I can stacking these shelves until 5:30 on my last day when I walk out of the building,' because personal pride dictates that's what you ought to do.

I think that's what's missing in so many people, whether it's the work that they do, their attitude on life, their attitude toward employers. I mean, the number of people who seem to think the world owes them a living now is unbelievable. I saw somebody on LinkedIn the other day giving themselves a pat on the back for working 40 hours a week for the last five years or something. And it's like, "Holy mother of god. I've not managed to do 40 hours a week in my entire life. If I get away with less than 70 hours, I'm doing pretty well."

My eldest son is 19, and he works in three of our businesses of his own volition. We didn't hold his feet to the fire or whatever. So technically, he's working seven days a week. But he's 19, and he can do that, can't he? Because he's loving the money he's earning and so on and so forth, and he only earns the same as his peers. And we have a restaurant and he works in there Friday and Saturday and sometimes Sunday evenings and he gets £7.50 an hour like the rest of the team. We don't pay him anymore because of who he is. But he's out there and his attitude is great, and it's just great to see.

So even if I wasn't here and he wasn't in the position he's in, I would bet money that he will be success at whatever it is that he decides to do.

What is the one book you'd recommend to every middle manager?

Because I think everything you do in life is a state of mind and the mind is a really powerful thing, I'd recommend The Chimp Paradox, by Steve Peters. I can't see how anybody can read that and not relate to themselves. So, you can relate to the fact we've all got a chimp, and occasionally, they get out of the box, and it's not very helpful

What question haven't I asked that you think I should have?

That's a good question, isn't it? That's a really good question. It's not often I'm lost for words, but the honest answer to that is I'm not sure.

I think a lot of people, find life is frustrating because they seem to think when you've done well in life somehow you walked along one day, found a bar of gold on the pavement, and suddenly that made life hunky dory for you. I think a lot of people misunderstand that. You can achieve all sorts of things in your life, and your definition of what great is can vary, can't it?

So maybe going full circle, one of the questions that you could've asked is 'what the definition of wealth is'. Because for different people, that might be how much money you've got in the bank, how big your house is, how many holidays you go on, and so on and so forth.

I still talk about a chap who used to work for me a number of years ago, and I still describe him as the wealthiest guy I ever knew. The reason I describe him like that was because he had the same job for 20 years. He worked 9:00 'till 5:00. From the business, he could see his house, and his wife used to bring his packed lunch across at lunchtime. He never worried about a thing in his life. He had no ambition in life, and he had everything he wanted in life. He had Cheryl his wife, David, his little boy, and he could see his house and walk to work. He was the wealthiest guy I knew because he just had everything he wanted.

For everybody else, you ask 20 people, you'll get 20 answers, won't you? But I think your definition of wealth is important. And I think for me, when I was younger, my definition of wealth was all the things that you would expect from a young, immature man, big house, big car, all these kinds of things. Then as I've got older, I've realised that my definition of wealth now really is time. And of course, creating monetary wealth and assets actually buys you time because you've got the freedom to choose what you do. You're not restricted to 22 days' holiday a year or you've got to be in at 8:30 and you've got to go home at 5:30 and so on and so forth.

So, the money, buys you the freedom to choose what you want to do with your time, and for me, that's the most valuable asset that you can possibly have.

What two things have struck you most from what was said?

What one thing will you do differently/employ as a result of what you've learnt from this chapter?

17

Lisa Quinn

Director - Founder & Director of Oaqgrove

Lisa is the founder and director of Oaqgrove, a not-for-profit enterprise - aimed at supporting government, public, not for profit, social and local organisations to achieve sustainable growth and transform and safeguard local communities. Prior to that she held director positions at Link Asset Services and Capita Asset Services. She was also the director of finance and business services at Cheshire East Council, the third largest authority in the North West.

What was your best memory or achievement as a middle manager?

As a middle manager in local government finance, my best memory is related to a brilliant team effort to replace a tired financial management system with a brand new shiny one. What stood out for me was the support that I had from both senior management and my team to be brave with our choice.

The system that met our requirements, from cost through to functionality, was a private sector system previously untested in local government. I am showing my age now, but the most exciting aspect was the direct link with

Microsoft products, the key one being Excel, which was not available in other tried and tested products at that time. All management reports could be automatically created in pre-designed spreadsheets. Forecasting previously done manually could be populated in minutes.

We had to make some tough decisions as a team along the way and deal with resistance to change, particularly when it came to new business processes, both within the team and across the authority. There is no doubt that the project was painful at times, and got in the way of the normal workload, which tested the patience of all to the absolute maximum.

To sum up, we were brave, and it was a huge challenge, but it was successful. It allowed finance professionals to move from labour intensive input to value added advice to the rest of the authority. It enabled a natural down-sizing in staffing and enabled the team to meet stricter deadlines for closure of accounts. The positive outcome exceeded our expectations, unbelievably satisfying.

Who was the best boss you ever had and why?

He was my first boss in local government, Principal Accountant and deputy Chief Financial Officer (CFO). I will never forget what he said to me in my interview, I was 19. If you take on this job and train hard you could be doing my job one day. That hit me like a bolt of lightning.

The outcome was......he trained me, both internally and externally, and promoted me along the way. He helped me to qualify as a public sector accountant, I was 28. He supported my development and I did get his job, I was 36. He paved the way for my progression, as he retired, and I became a Director of Finance two years later, I was 38. Need I say more..........

What was the greatest challenge you faced as a middle manager?

My greatest challenge was something that seemed incredibly unfair at the time but had to be professionally and calmly managed. One of the things that you do not wish to happen in your career as a Finance Manager is for the external auditor to turn around and say, at the very last minute, that they are not prepared to sign off the accounts. That is what happened to me and my team.

We understood why they had made the decision, but we had done all we could to manage a new accounting requirement in the time we had. The perceived unfairness came in the form of inconsistent approach. Others that were in a similar position to us still had their accounts signed off in time, with actions to be undertaken to resolve the situation in the following year.

What got me and my team through this challenging time was the support of senior management and political leadership at the local authority. The accounts were signed off eventually and there were no adverse implications for the future. It turned out well, but it was extremely upsetting at its worst.

What was the biggest mistake you made when you were a middle manager?

As I became deputy CFO, and my predecessor was handing over, I supported the appointment of someone internally as a team manager on what seemed was a logical basis. It was part of a restructure and this person's previous role and experience seemed to fit.

However, I was being naive to the history amongst the team, who had worked alongside each other for many years, and the mix of personalities. Consequently, there were many challenging situations in the office, some confrontations being very difficult and had to be dealt with by one of my reporting managers.

I had progressed through the organisation over the years, at first junior to many of the team that I then ended up managing. I had learned much about the business requirements, but I had some way to go in understanding what makes people tick. This was not about competency, they were all very good at their jobs, it was about who should manage and who is willing to be managed.

The reason I mention this situation is that I met one of my former team very recently, having not seen them for a few years. This was someone older than me that I grew up with at work, looked after me at times, and someone that I very much respect. They recounted this situation to me and it brought it home that it mattered, and it had been the wrong decision for all concerned.

I think it is easy as a middle manager to take what seems to be the straight-forward route of appointing internally, when the better decision would be to recruit externally or at least re-think the structure.

What personal qualities do you see in the best middle managers?

Resilience – you will face challenges from above, you will need to be a buffer to protect your team at times and you will need to support your team – this requires resilience

Kind – in my view this should come naturally as a leader and does not mean that you are not an assertive or strong leader, quite the opposite

Sense of humour – I could not get by without having fun along the way – having a laugh with your team shows that you are human and is a great stress reliever – it can also break down barriers with other colleagues, when appropriate

Supportive – especially when things go wrong – I have found that you will receive as much support as you give, which creates an inspiring atmosphere

Collaborative – it is easy to become protective of your team and not reach out to other colleagues and teams, as it is can be challenging to collaborate – however, I have found that most of my best outcomes as a middle manager came from effective collaboration – it has led to life-long friendships

Brave – do not be afraid of being the first to do something or of failing – this can differentiate you for future opportunities and can lead to greater learning and insights

What skills do you think middle managers should focus on developing to ensure their effectiveness over their career?

Negotiation – you will need to apply strong negotiation skills to all the things that you do as a middle manager – partly due to lack of overall control as a manager and a general need to compromise to make progress

Mediation – we all know that not everything goes according to plan and you will need to deal with many personality traits in your team – you will need to learn when to mediate yourself and when you need support for mediation.

Diplomacy – when dealing with senior management I have found that diplomacy is a very effective skill – this does not mean giving in and compromising too much, it means having an understanding of internal politics and how best to contribute positively and constructively in any given circumstance.

Team psychology – I am not a big fan of personality tests. However, whatever method you use make sure that you understand the individuals in your team as far as they will let you. Know their strengths and weaknesses and work out which members of your team are capable and willing to be taken out of their comfort zone.

Above all, lead by example, don't get lost in your status and stay grounded.

What do you know now that you wish you knew as a middle manager?

That sometimes you cannot make a situation better and you have to move on, physically and mentally. That loyalty and dedication is not always rewarded in the workplace and you should consider the impact on your personal life, as well as your work life.

That flexibility and freedom is possible when working full time, both for yourself and for your team. That getting to the top of your profession can be lonely, so be prepared.

Having said all that, I wouldn't change it for the world!

What's your one Tip for the Top?

Get your greatest satisfaction from the achievement of the people that support you.

What is the one book you'd recommend to every middle manager?

I must admit, even though I am contributing to this worthy publication, I am not one for leadership and management books. My recommendation is therefore slightly different. In my view, a good thing to do is to read the book that you remember most fondly from your younger days.

Make time to read it again now and see what impact it has on you. In my case, middle management sometimes dulled my true self. Immersing yourself in the things that inspired you in life at the start of your career can be a real tonic for the here and now. It may be a small thing, but it could contribute to renewed motivation to make the breakthrough that you are striving to achieve.

Break the mould and move on and up.

What question haven't I asked that you think I should have?

What motivated you to strive for the top?

My ambition grew with each role that I took on. I thought that I was technical until I was given the opportunity to manage. I thought that I had to re-examine my career until an unexpected opportunity came up. I thought that I would remain a middle manager until I was given the opportunity to lead, and I love it.

What two things have struck you most from what was said?

What one thing will you do differently/employ as a result of what you've learnt from this chapter?

18

Martin Ellis

Former Regional Managing Director, EMEA, Rentokil

Now a headhunter, Martin considers himself very fortunate to have spent his entire career working in meritocracies, especially at Rentokil Initial where he started as a Marketing Assistant and ended responsible for one fifth of the company's revenue, and a quarter of it's profits. He lived and worked all over Europe, North America, Asia and Africa as one of the organisation's five Regional Managing Directors. That experience is invaluable in assessing candidates for senior leadership roles. He runs the Executive Search desk for the RSE Group.

What was the greatest challenge you faced as a middle manager?

Being micromanaged. I made sure I had mentors who would help me through that and guided me through to an understanding of leadership, as well as management.

What was the biggest mistake you made when you were a middle manager?

I discovered that trying to be fair to everybody around me was counter-productive. I made decisions in isolation, and those watching me from a distance thought the very opposite of what I intended. Only when I tried to be consistent, did decision making become easier and people could see the consistency and understood where they stood in the organisation.

What personal qualities do you see in the best middle managers?

They share goals, targets, and visions and get their people to understand them and buy into them.

They get enough information to make informed decisions quickly. They don't dither.

They make more good decisions than bad.

They don't make the same mistake twice.

They don't micromanage from behind a closed door.

They celebrate success.

They never belittle people in front of an audience.

They understand their numbers.

They smile a lot.

They are often funny.

They listen to people. They do not have to agree with them, but they have to be able to explain why they don't, if they don't

What skills do you think middle managers should focus on developing to ensure their effectiveness over their career?

Sales skills. People skills. Presentation and communication skills.

How to read a P&L, and how the balance sheet can tell you more about what's really happening in your organisation and how your customers regard you.

How the informal company network operates. Who are the voices that hold sway?

THE BIG ONE: Learn how to manage managers.

What do you know now that you wish you knew as a middle manager?

That you shouldn't do subordinates jobs for them. That feeds down through the organisation, and everybody spends too much time looking over his or her shoulders.

What's your one Tip for the Top?

Work on your current job only. Make a success of that and you will be promoted.

What is the one book you'd recommend to any and every middle manager?

The One-Minute Manager and the One-Minute Salesman. Both simple books that form a good foundation for what is to follow. Also read The Economist to keep in touch with the world.

Who was the best boss you ever had and why?

I've had some excellent bosses. Often they would tell me that something couldn't be done – and I couldn't resist the challenge. They also asked a lot of me, gave me responsibility, celebrated success, and helped ensure I didn't repeat my failures. They gave me space to do my job, but didn't orphan me. They were often very funny and made hard times enjoyable.

What question haven't I asked that you think I should have?

"Did you learn anything from you worse boss?"
   I still carry my worse bosses in my pocket. If I am stuck, I wonder what they would do. I then do the polar opposite. It usually works.

What two things have struck you most from what was said?

What one thing will you do differently/employ as a result of what you've learnt from this chapter?

19

Matthew Dashper-Hughes

Founder, OPS Office Supplies and former COO, Rymans Stationary, Managing Director Bargain Booze

What was the greatest challenge you faced as a middle manager?

A desire to be liked.

That might sound like an odd answer, but it is a painfully honest one.

The secret to management of others is the management of oneself. For me that meant, to an extent, overcoming my innate need to be liked; to realise that life is not a popularity contest!

It took me a long time to understand my own strengths and weaknesses, and to realise that, in some circumstances, a trait that would otherwise be a strength can become a weakness.

My personality profile is that of an outgoing extrovert, with a high need for personal approval. Secondary characteristics in my profile include a high focus on people and caring. It's not until you get to my tertiary characteristics that you see the more typical 'CEO' traits – bluntness, decisiveness, intolerance of time wasting etc.

So, the things I had to learn in the early days were mainly about recognising when I was being too nice, and to channel my inner CEO. Then, of course, I had to learn when I was going too far the other way – maybe even sending mixed messages to my team by being unintentionally 'Jekyll and Hyde'.

The best lessons I learnt were around how to provide clarity. Giving a clear framework and strong communication of vision and strategic goals, so that members of the team could always understand the context for the tasks they were being asked to perform.

People tend to perform better when they are engaged, and they buy into not only what you are doing as a business or a team, but also why you are doing it!

What was the biggest mistake you made when you were a middle manager?

Like a lot of people who get into management, I sort of fell into it by accident.

I was promoted to a managerial position back in the year 2000, not because I showed an aptitude for management, but because I was good at the job I was already doing. Which was something totally different. It was like being asked to be an astronaut because I happened to be good at making spacesuits!

For that reason, in the early days, I made a huge number of mistakes until I realised that the best managers get things done, whilst the worst managers do things themselves.

In that sense, I was a bad manager in the early days!

That is not to say that a manager should delegate everything and do nothing him or herself. Far from it – leading by example and never asking anyone to do anything you are not prepared to do yourself can be a profoundly strong managerial tool.

However, effective delegation, goal setting, task metrics, clearly defined role expectations and clarity of communication are the essential ingredients in the manager's cookbook.

What personal qualities do you see in the best middle managers?

Emotional intelligence. An understanding of how different people's minds work, and a clear ability to communicate effectively with different colleagues – both upwards and downwards in the hierarchy – dependent upon their personal styles.

What skills do you think middle managers should focus on developing to ensure their effectiveness over their career?

To be an effective manager you need to be a coach, a counsellor, a leader, an operator, and a psychologist.

In other words, you need to be an empathetic chameleon with fabulous communication skills.

The best advice I could give to anyone starting out in management is, firstly, to recognise that it is a different job to any you have had before. Running a team is not the same as being part of a team.

Develop your understanding of how other people communicate, how they think, and how you can get the best out of them. Invest in personal development for yourself – some management training and also some EQ based psychometrics such as Smart Insights or DISC profiling.

What do you know now that you wish you knew as a middle manager?

Probably the clue to that is in some of my previous answers!

If there was one thing I could point to as a specific example of where I got it wrong in the early days, it would be around recruitment.

I made the classic mistake of recruiting whilst desperate to fill a position. It's like going to the supermarket whilst you are hungry – you fill your trolley full of crap!

So, what I wish I had known sooner was how to utilise an effective process to recruit for people.

Lessons would be:

1. If you are desperate to fill a position and the candidate is desperate for a new role, chances are the results will also be pretty desperate.
2. Start your process with the CV, by all means, but also get the candidate to fill in your own form. Alternatively, do a quick telephone interview to qualify the candidate for a proper interview. Don't rely purely on the CV.
3. Depending on the position, consider getting your shortlist of candidates to do a psychometric profiling exercise to assess their strengths and weaknesses.
4. Don't just interview on a competency basis – cultural fit is at least as important as skill set … maybe more so!
5. When you have hired someone, that is when the real work starts. Make sure their first few weeks are very clearly mapped out and that you have regular weekly review sessions with them, at which you look at how they are performing against clearly defined metrics. You can weed out the bad hires very quickly!

What's your one Tip for the Top?

Surround yourself with good people and have the confidence to let them do their jobs. Especially if they are better at something than you are!

What is the one book you'd recommend to any and every middle manager?

'Endurance' by Alfred Lansing. It's a 1959 biography of Ernest Shackleton's voyage to the South Pole. When you read it, you cannot help but marvel at the techniques he used to maintain his crew's engagement, and to get them all home safely after disaster befell the Endurance. The whole story is remarkable but is also an object lesson in how to manage people through clarity of communication and clearly defined task allocation.

Who was the best boss you ever had and why?

I am lucky – I have worked for some truly impressive and gifted people.

Unluckily that makes this a very hard question to answer – I have picked up different skills, approaches, and 'dos and don'ts' from all of them, so asking me to choose is very tough!

I will have to answer, I think, in terms of 'The Boss I Would Like to be Most Similar to', and that would be Darcy Wilson-Rymer, whom I worked for on a six-month project back in 2013.

Darcy is the ex-CEO of Starbucks UK, so he has a strong corporate background and is a professional manager and a great public speaker. I worked for him not long after he had taken the reins at Costcutter. He's a profoundly decent and generous man, with strong emotional intelligence, and an ability to get the best out of people through engagement.

I witnessed him leading from the front during a period of significant cultural and operational change, and it was like being treated to a masterclass in how to keep a team of colleagues thoroughly engaged and 'switched on'.

He was also remarkably generous with his time and his insights and I came away a better operator because of my time with him.

What question haven't I asked that you think I should have?

The only key question that we haven't explored is that of the differences between management and leadership.

There's an old saying that accountants live in the past, managers live in the present, and leaders live in the future.

What that means is that the business of the finance department is usually reporting on what has happened, managers are usually dealing with the tactical stuff of day-to-day operations, whilst leaders set the strategic direction and the vision for the business.

This is, of course, a gross oversimplification. The best operators in all three fields incorporate a little of everything into their suite of skills.

The most effective managers are those that are good at leading as well as managing. Managers have to give their team jobs to do. It's a role that is largely defined by getting tasks completed and delivering expected results. However, the leadership aspect of the role comes in daily reinforcement and communication of cultural and visionary context for behaviours and tasks. Often this involves using the company's values as a set of touchstones to underpin actions.

What two things have struck you most from what was said?

What one thing will you do differently/employ as a result of what you've learnt from this chapter?

20

Paul Lyons

Managing Director, Mental Toughness Partners

Paul Lyons is an experienced recruitment business leader, adviser and coach on leadership and mental toughness.

He assists recruitment business owners and leaders to develop their personal and business leadership skills and grow their business.

He has 25 years CEO experience, currently as Interim Managing Partner of the iconic Australian executive search firm Watermark. Before that he spent 15 years as co-founder and CEO of the ASX listed company, Ambition, following on from 10 years as Managing Director Australia and Asia Pacific for Michael Page International.

He has also established Mental Toughness Partners, an international network of practitioners assisting individuals and organisations in building their mindset and mental toughness.

What was your best memory or achievement as a middle manager?

I think my greatest success was to have played a part in building two high calibre teams of people within the sizeable and successful businesses that were Michael Page International Asia Pacific and Ambition.

My greatest setback was abruptly leaving Ambition in 2013. However in looking for the positive I was able to use that intense disappointment and drive by developing a keen interest in the power of the 4Cs Mental Toughness framework. I then established Mental Toughness Partners, an international network of practitioners assisting individuals and organisations in building their mindset and mental toughness.

Who was the best boss you ever had and why?

No question – Terry Benson, Group CEO at Michael Page based in London when I was Australian and then Asia Pacific Managing Director based in Sydney and subsequently Hong Kong. Terry was charismatic and so you wanted to work for him. He was good at keeping complex things simple, gave you lots of rope but kept you very accountable to your goals and targets. He also was perceptive at knowing when it was the right time to give you a new challenge.

What was the greatest challenge you faced as a middle manager?

As with most middle managers, I was responsible for achieving outcomes through managing a team of people and managing a process. I struggled most with the balance of team time and my time; if I spent too much time with my team, I struggled to complete my own work but if I spent too much time on my work, my team suffered.

What was the biggest mistake you made when you were a middle manager?

My influencing skills were non-existent. It was my way or the highway. If telling them didn't work I just shouted louder!

What personal qualities do you see in the best middle managers?

I think the best middle managers are already leaders in waiting. They possess a resilient and positive mindset and are proficient at managing the complexity, which is required as a manager. They are already developing their vision, their strategic thinking and their influencing and coaching skills.

What skills do you think middle managers should focus on developing to ensure their effectiveness over their career?

As per above it is important to over achieve as a manager but to also show potential as a leader. The more trust you can develop with your manager and board the more responsibility they will give you.

What do you know now that you wish you knew as a middle manager?

The art of listening more and talking less. Listening is an underrated but critically important skill, especially when combined with smart questions that get other people speaking about their motivations, situations and specific intentions . You learn much more listening than you ever can by talking.

Do what you say you are going to do. This is critical to build the trust and rapport you will need to succeed in any role including that as a middle manager. It never ceases to amaze me the number of people that promise something but fail to deliver, which leads to a breakdown in trust over time.

What's your one Tip for the Top?

There are three.

Firstly, keep your purpose front and centre. When you are a manager, thinking time is at a premium and it is easy to lose track of the months and years and suddenly wake up one day disillusioned and just going through the motions. If that happens, it means that you have lost touch with your dreams and your 'why'. Your purpose that gets you up in the morning fully charged and ready to go. You need to ensure that you always know with clarity and confidence what your purpose is and that you keep it front and centre as your career and life navigational star.

Secondly, become adept at managing managers. The mark of a good leader is being able to lead a team through a group of managers, which means your message has to be clear and your style consistent.

Lastly, be adaptable. It is more important to be employable than employed. Ensure that you stay marketable by being adaptable and flexible in acquiring new skills and responding to change.

What is the one book you'd recommend to every middle manager?

Since I believe passionately in the power of purpose and its importance as a guiding light and driver , the one book I would recommend is 'Start with Why' by Simon Sinek . In the book Sinek explains that people are inspired by a sense of purpose (or "Why") and that this should come first, before How and What.

What two things have struck you most from what was said?

What one thing will you do differently/employ as a result of what you've learnt from this chapter?

21

Peter Freeth

Author, Speaker, Talent Coach

Peter started work in 1985, as an apprentice in a IT company. He went on to hold a variety of technical, team leader and sales roles in mostly big corporates in manufacturing, systems integrators and carriers.

Over the last 17 years Peter has run his own consultancy, working with mostly mid-sized to global corporates on talent and leadership programs, leadership development, executive coaching. Three or four times a year Peter runs NLP training which, "allows me to continually develop what I do and come up with new ideas, and innovate". Then I take that into the coaching or the corporate classroom." He is the author of 14 books including NLP for Business, Plain Selling, Change Magic and Building Your Career Capital.

What was your best memory or achievement as a middle manager?

I'm interpreting the label of middle manager through the whole of my career really.

I think it's very easy for managers to get into the rut of measuring their value by how they're measured. There's an American company I work with, and the only thing they measure is sales results. So it's very easy for people get into the way of thinking that the only value they add is through contributing to the sales results. But their contribution is minimal really. Their sale process is so complex and the way that the customer-seller relationship has changed over the last 20 years has put the buyer much more in an informed position, a position of control. The salesperson is really just along for the ride a lot of the time. Or they're there to manage the complexity of the supplier organisation, they're not really there to sell anything.

There's a whole lot of superstition, a huge amount of fear of failure when it comes to working with people who are middle to senior level managers. The thing which I always get the biggest sense of achievement from isn't somebody coming back and saying, "Yeah, we hit our quarterly sales target."

They could have sat on their hands and probably hit it because customer demand creates a momentum. They're not pushing customers along from scratch, the marketplace is creating momentum. It's when they talk about doing very, very simple things, like starting to delegate, and then they come back a month later and they're amazed at how simple it's been and how effective it's been.

Recently a client released half a day a week, so that's 10% of his working life he's got back just by delegating. Everything that needs to happen in his team has still happened. A second client freed up one day a week, that's 20% of his time. The irony is we send managers on courses like strategic thinking and leadership but they won't use any of those skills because they don't have the time to use them. They think "oh, those are some really good tips or techniques, I'll try that next time I have time." They never have time. That's the root cause of the problem.

What I find interesting is as soon as you create time, the very, very first thing that people do is they step back and they think "hmm, what shall I do this week?" That's strategic thinking. Planning is strategic thinking. It seems that as soon as we create the time, that comes naturally, and when they're thinking about very long-term strategy, they might need some help to structure how they articulate that to the team. Fundamentally though, know how to do it. Another client I've been coaching said he went the entire weekend and didn't check his emails once.

That's the corporate world, a lot of these people feel under a lot of pressure, they're on 24 hours a day. They're working across multiple time zones and they're expected to be in conference calls from 6:00am through to 10:00pm, if that suits the people they're in a conference call with. They spend a lot of their time just on conference calls listening to broadcasts. It's like listening to the radio, from the headquarters, broadcasting sales information and updates and so on, and most of their time is spent just passing on information and not actually adding any value to it, not doing anything.

The client that said he didn't check his emails over the weekend was because he felt comfortable and he felt safe that he knew that his team had everything under control.

Something that I thought of looking at several of your questions was 'What is the fundamental job of a manager?' It is to delegate. If you think about an organisational structure or hierarchy, and the way we normally draw an organisational structure, we've got all the authority starting at the top because if you imagine you're self-employed, you do everything yourself. You do the thing that you do, plus you do sales and marketing and websites and finance and accounts.

All of that authority is in one person, and as you start a business and start to hire other people, you start to delegate that authority to others. You say, "You're in charge of finance, you're in charge of admin, you're in charge of sales," whatever. The organisation, whether it's one person, or in this case, 22,000 people, the fundamental job of a manager is to delegate authority, and through that, to add value and to delegate it to the most appropriate people, and to develop people's skills around what's been delegated to them.

When managers make themselves roadblocks it's because they feel under pressure, to deliver something, to be doing something, and that's a very common issue I think.

So for me I wouldn't say there was one big standout memory or achievement, I think it's a series of things. It's been a shift in my focus to get people to free up time.

Then a number of things have to happen. First they have to use that time for something new, and to relax, to get control of their lives back, to spend more time with their families, spend more time doing the things that enjoy doing, that give them the energy to bring to work, to do the job that they're paid to do.

Secondly, in order to delegate all of that, somebody else has got to be doing it. That means the team are now focusing on tasks which are at a higher level of authority. That's interesting for them, it's challenging for them, they're learning new skills, they're developing in their careers because the best way to move on in your career is do your boss's job. Demand that your boss delegates more to you. Now automatically you're working at a higher organisational level.

I think any time that I've been able to help a client do that, they say, "I can't believe what a difference it's made, it seemed like such a simple thing to do." An interesting point is that they all think they're already doing it. They all think they're already good at delegating, but what most managers do is they delegate tasks. This isn't helpful because what they do is they stand over somebody, tell them what to do to achieve the task, and then watch them do it. Then they think, "Well that took ages, I may as well do it myself". The person they delegated the task to didn't learn anything from it, they were just following instructions, so it didn't help anybody.

What they've got to do is delegate authority, and specify the end result, and then they leave that person to figure out how to get the end result for themselves. I like to describe good delegation as a series of controlled mistakes.

A manager that creates an environment that's safe and puts boundaries and limits on that authority so that a person can be free to make decisions in order to achieve the results, but can get it wrong will always achieve more.

One memory that does stand out is a client who was a country manager for one of the countries in Asia. These managers are starting off doing a lot of their team's work for them. They go into meetings with them, they're doing stuff with them and their people are not learning anything from it. It's just duplication of effort.

My mantra to them is delegate everything, knowing, or expecting at least, that most of the managers will take that with a pinch of salt and think "I'll delegate a few things, but I can't delegate everything." But at least if they believe they've got to delegate everything, they will delegate more than they would than if I said, "Oh, just delegate what you can. Delegate what you think is appropriate." You're always going to limit, so not delegating becomes the default.

Anyway, this country manager totally took it to heart, jumped off the deep end and delegated everything. I spoke to him the month later and I said, "How did it go?" He said, "Yeah, I took your advice, I delegated everything."

He just went for it. I wasn't expecting that. I said, "What happened?" He said, "Actually, they really screwed up a project, a customer project, and we made a huge mistake." I was thinking "Oh my God!" I asked "Okay, and how do you feel about that?" He said, "Actually, really good because they learnt so much from it, and it was much better that they screwed up a small project now than a big one later."

What he created was the psychological safety for his team to fail. The psychological safety he created comes from the limitation of the scope of authority that's been delegated. It's like putting a playpen round a child, they could do whatever they want, they can play with whatever they want, so actually, they don't feel penned in, they feel free because they're doing whatever they want to do. Because of course, a barrier always works two ways, it keeps in, but it also keeps out as well.

We put the playpen up to keep the child in, but also maybe to keep the dog out. We build fences to keep things out, but then if people are aware of what's on the other side and they want to go off and explore, they might feel hemmed in by that.

The job of the manager in that regard is to create limits or boundaries within which a team can make a series of controlled mistakes, because that's the thing that will accelerate their experiential learning the most. We must give them that primary experience of failing and nothing bad really happening as a result.

There was another client in India who was responsible for a huge part of the business. He had about 400 people working for him, directly and indirectly, and the only thing he was measured on every month was orders and shipments.

Every month, coming to the end of the month or quarter, he would get more and more stressed, give up more and more of his free time, his weekends were gone, pushing out every order, every shipment, every task and process that he could to make sure he hit that target, because he was afraid of what would happen if he didn't. His manager would say to him, "Oh, don't you dare fail, don't you dare miss that target."

In years of doing this job he'd never once asked the question, "What's going to happen?" One quarter, he decided to do an experiment, which was a bit scary. He was just going to sit on his hands and not do anything. If something was progressing normally, he would progress it, but he wasn't going to push anything. He decided he wouldn't work evenings and weekends. He just let it all flow along at the pace dictated by all the other people in the organisation who were involved.

What happened was that he hit one target and just missed another, and then he had a primary experience of missing the target and his manager didn't even mention it to him. Nothing happened. He realised all these years he'd been stressing out about these targets and the fear of failing, and nobody really cared about them.

Who's the best boss you've ever had and why? And who's the best boss you've ever seen?

That's an interesting way of looking at it. I thought of two people. The first was a guy when I first got into pre-sales, and he was a sales manager at Mercury Communications, which was part of Cable & Wireless. His name was Paul, and I worked in the specialist sales team. My job was helping the sales people translate technical customer requirements into network designs and service designs, pricing and tender responses and stuff like that. It was the technical side of the sales team.

One of the specialist banking account teams wanted me to go and work for them, and they offered me a job over there, and I was flattered and interested in it, and so I went and spoke to Paul about it. He took me for lunch and just talked it over in a very neutral way, and said, "Well, this is the way I see it, and these are the advantages of this and these are the advantages of that, and I think this is the kind of person you are and the sort of things you're interested in." But I never felt that he was pushing me to do one thing or another. I think he wanted me to stay in his team, but I never felt pushed into that. I never felt that I was being forced into a decision.

The deal was that if I stayed in the team, he'd buy lunch, and if I moved then I'd buy lunch. I decided to stay on the basis that he'd seen something, he recognised something in me. He saw that one of the things I enjoyed most was variety because variety creates the most opportunities for learning, and I would have a lot more variety in the specialist team than in an account team.

It was the right decision, but it was an interesting process to go through, and I really felt like what he did was make the choice clearer for me, but ultimately it was my choice and my responsibility.

Then I had a client who had an executive search business. They had offices all over the world, and every year they would all get together somewhere and have a joint company holiday and strategy development session. This would last about a week. I went along to do some team building stuff with them. The way it worked was that I created a series of challenges, not for team building, but actually to create conflict, in order to reproduce some of the things that were happening in the office that they weren't dealing with, and that were actually impacting on their performance.

They can do everything right and still fail. They were very ineffective at dealing with the intense frustration that comes from that, because they were generally ex-bankers or ex-journalists, and somewhat egotistical.

They didn't deal well with failure, especially when they felt like that success was somehow owed to them because they'd worked so hard for it.

There was one challenge where it was basically like a talent show. They had to go out into the streets of Istanbul and find a stranger, and convince them to come to this big, lavish party in the evening. Then they would present this person and talk about their lives, and make them an interesting story.

I then had to judge the winning team, and one of the teams that didn't win were incredibly aggrieved by this. There was a Chinese lady who was the head of the team in Hong Kong who was incredibly aggrieved, and this English guy was so angry that I hadn't chosen his team. There was this huge fallout, and it almost turned into a physical fight. It was intensely uncomfortable.

The owner of the business, John, just stood back and let it all happen, and it just degenerated into this horrible atmosphere. What was interesting was I reflected on what had happened and felt under pressure to change my decision. The other teams said, "Well, it's your decision. You chose it for a reason, if you change it, now you're going to piss somebody else off."

I realised they were right so I stuck with it and I apologised to these two people for upsetting them with my decision.

The Chinese lady was absolutely delighted that I'd apologised, and thus allowed her to save face. She was my best friend on the trip after that and sat next to me at dinner. The English guy wouldn't make eye contact with me. It was almost like the apology compounded the insult.

But then the owner of the business, in his reflecting in the aftermath of all of this, gave me probably the best piece of advice I've ever had in my working life, which was, "It's not your job to be liked."

That one piece of advice transformed the work that I do and the way I work with clients, and now creating conflict is something I do quite often. Actually, I'll often start a new coaching relationship by saying, "I'm always on your side, but sometimes it might not feel like that."

I say to clients, "There are times that you're going to feel like you're making progress and this is going to be great, there are going to be times when you'll think I hate this, I want this to stop. Because you're going to feel uncomfortable, and in order for you to do the things that you haven't done before, you're going to have to go through some discomfort to get there. I'll help you minimise that as much as possible, but ultimately it's you that's got to do that, not me."

I think that understanding is one of the most important things for coaches to grasp. I see many coaches who are desperately trying to get into rapport with a client, and be nice and be on their side, and they don't see how ineffective that is. What a disservice they're doing to the client by trying to protect the client from that discomfort and actually protect themselves from that discomfort.

One of the things I teach, particularly on training relevant to coaching, is you've got to be comfortable with discomfort. Because if you're not, then the client is going to find it much harder in the long runt to get to where they want to be. It's the same for managers. If they want their teams to develop they have to be prepared to feel uncomfortable, to not be popular sometimes but with the goal that they help their people develop.

What's the greatest challenge you faced when you were in management, and what's the greatest challenge, you think, facing managers now?

It's an interesting distinction because I think a lot of people talk about the challenges of managing millennials, of managing a geographically diverse team or of integrating technology into the way they manage and so on. But these are all temporary challenges. I think what managers are always faced with is human nature, and I think the biggest challenge is dealing with bullying and conflict within a team.

I've actually had a situation recently where there was bullying going on within the HR team of all places. Somebody, who had been on long-term sick leave, was back, and was being ostracised by one person. This person was using the victim, if I can use that language, as a pawn in her attempt to actually put stress on the head of HR, who's job she thought she should have gotten. This was in order to create stress for him to the point that he would leave the job and that she thought that then, by definition, she would get the job. She drew the whole team into this black hole of her own making. I think that's what bullies do they project out the pain that's going on inside. Now she is manipulating people in the team around her as part of the game.

At the surface, you can't see it. You talk to any one person and it all seems to make sense. You understand things, if you're trying to understand things from the person's point of view, but it's only when you put them all together in a room together and light the blue touch paper, that you actually see those interactions play out for real. Then you see what's going on, and that's intensely uncomfortable.

I think the easiest thing to do, and what the head of HR had been doing, is run away from it. Brush it under the carpet, just get through the day, don't deal with it, but it just gets bigger and bigger.

He had an expectation from the half day that we spent on it, that it would be the end of it, everything would be resolved and everybody would be happier. Actually, what we were left with is an intensely uncomfortable position, where the perpetrator had been exposed and now she's in a very, very difficult position. Because, without intending to and without realising it, she's put all her cards on the table.

Now all the people who perhaps have previously been her allies, or at least ambivalent to her behaviour, can now see what she's doing, everyone knows what she's up to.

I have another client, who has got an under-performer in his team, he's not doing a whole load of things and the manager is repeatedly telling him, "Look, you've got to do these things, these things are mandatory. Other people do these things."

What he's not doing is getting this person to take responsibility by saying, "If you continue to not do these things, you will lose your job." He's standing over the person, like a parent, saying, "You've got to do this, you've got to do that etc." The person doesn't know why he has to do that. Other than he's been told to by his manager and he'll continue to fight against that. His mindset is "I've been told I've got to do this and I don't see why I should have to do this."

My client sent the guy a copy of the policies and said, "Look, it's in the policies," and somewhere hidden deep within the policies, it implies in a roundabout way that not doing this thing is a serious offence. He's hoping that the guy's going to read into that and take it seriously. He's never actually explicitly said to him, "This is what will happen if you carry on doing this."

I pointed it out to him that it's not his decision. If his team member has got all the information, and the consequences have been explained to him, then he's made the decision. If, with that information, he carries on doing what he's doing he's made the decision to accept the consequences.

He's chosen he doesn't want to play by the rules of the team. Well that's okay, that's his choice, but he doesn't get to do that and still be part of the team.

We talked about a feeling of responsibility and that this guy's got a family, and I said, "Well you mustn't forget that's his responsibility. You can't allow him to push that onto you, and use that to coerce you into keeping the situation going."

I think the other thing that's very easy for managers to forget is that they focus on the one individual, who may be the star or the under-performer, and they don't see how that narrow focus has an impact on the rest of the team. Actually causing disengagement in the rest of the team is a far bigger problem than the under-performance of one person.

I think that's the biggest challenge managers face, their reluctance to deal with human nature. It comes back to what I said about delegation. The manager thinking they've got to sort it all out and not seeing it from the point of view that people are here because they made a choice to be here. If they decide they don't want to be here anymore, then that's fine, that's up to them. But they don't get to be in the team and enjoy the benefits of being in the team, but not play by the rules of the team. Once you allow one person to do that, now everybody's doing that. Now the team has fallen apart and as the manager, your job's threatened because the whole team's ineffective.

I think millennials have a slightly tough time because they have perhaps unrealistic expectations of the workplace that have been created by universities. They've been saying, "You're the best. Employers are going to be falling over themselves to hire you, they're going to give you these amazing careers."

Some universities are being extremely unfair and unrealistic in the picture they paint, and with highly vocational degrees you're expected to come out of that degree course with sometimes a specific job with a specific employer. The reality is that they are turning out more and more potential employees than there are jobs in that industry. How would you behave if you had been systematically lied to for three years, and then you find out it's not at all how it's been presented to you? The problem isn't the way people behave at work, the problem is the misalignment between two different systems. We've got people with one set of expectations pouring into a system that has very different expectations. You're going to see conflict.

If everybody had a millennial attitude and mindset, whatever that is, there wouldn't be a problem. It's the fact that we have this change in expectations, and this has changed with every generation. It changed with us when we started work. We think about some of the things that people said to us, "Oh, you expect everything on a plate, oh, you expect me to do the job for you, oh, you never learn. You'll calm down once you've learned a thing or two." We were told to "take things at your own pace, do what you're told, don't show initiative", because that's the generation they were coming from.

What personal qualities do you see in best managers?

Ownership and measurement.

For example, one of the things I do in my work is model high performers. I interview and observe the behaviour of, and get inside the head of high performers to figure out what it is they're doing differently to the average. That then gets turned into development programs, recruitment systems and so on. Whenever I am looking at high performing managers, there's something that comes up time and time again.

For example, let's take retail store managers. Head office create some change in policy or some new thing they've got to do, and the average retail store manager has their weekly team meeting and says, "Oh, we've been told we've got to do this by head office. I don't like it any more than you do, we've got no choice, we've got to do it." What the manager does is they put themselves in the safety of their team and they make head office the enemy.

From the team's point of view, the manager isn't part of the team. They see the manager as a representative of the company.

High performing managers do it differently. When they get a directive that they don't agree with, they think, "Well, they haven't taken that into account or these local conditions, or the size of my store," or whatever it might be. They call up their boss, the and say, "This is rubbish, I don't agree with this, this isn't going to work because ..." They have that debate with their manager.

Sometimes their manager says, "Oh, that's an interesting point. We haven't thought about that. Okay, hold fire, I'll go back," and sometimes the regional manager says, "Well I totally understand where you're coming from, but it is what it is and it's what you've got to do it." They say, "Oh, okay." Now they go back to their team and what they don't say is, "We've been told we've got to this by head office. I don't like it." They do say, "Here's what we need to do. From Monday, I want you to..."

They feel the conflict but they externalise it, they channel it appropriately and they change it if they can. If they can't, it's part of them accepting that they have delegated responsibility. It's them asking their team to do it, not anybody else. They take ownership and if there's a problem, it's their problem to sort out. And because of that they are very clear about what other people are responsible for as well. That's ownership.

Then measurement. They know what to measure to get the results they want. You can't set out to improve anything, you can only change something and then measure what happens. If it changes in the direction that you want to go in, then keep going, and if it doesn't, you change direction.

What I find the best managers do is they develop their own measurements systems, and they use that measurement to tell them what's going on, to tell them how things are in the team, and if the team are performing. If we use retail store managers in the supermarket as an example, the average managers, if they wanted to know if something had been done, they'd go and ask the person who was supposed to do it. They would invariably say, "Yeah, I'm doing it, I'm doing it." Meaning I wasn't doing it, but you've just reminded me.

Or they would go and check the thing that was supposed to have been done, like checking best before dates, which means now two people have checked it, so it's duplication of effort. What the best managers do is to set up a log book so that when the staff do a certain routine task, they then sign the log book to say they've done it. The best managers would walk five or six paces outside their office and look in the log book, because they didn't see filling in the log book as something that's done after the task, filling in the logbook is the task, so the record and the measurement is the task. Now the member of staff has got to do the thing to then record it in the book. If you haven't put in the logbook, you haven't done the task.

The best managers made sure that measurement is part of the task.

What skills do you think managers should focus on developing to ensure their effectiveness over the career?

We've got to understand what the essential role of the manager is. It's to delegate authority. To divide up and delegate authority so that the work gets distributed in the most appropriate and efficient way.

I think the most important and most valuable skill for managers to develop is delegating, and I think most managers are very bad at it. They think they're delegating tasks and they're good at telling people what to do, and that's not delegating. Delegating is about giving people the authority to do something. I use the acronym AIR in management training to explain this.

You've got to give your team AIR if you want them to perform. Give them space, give them room to do what they do. AIR stands for Authority, Information, Result. Give them the authority and the information to make the decisions that are necessarily in achieving a result. You've got to be very specific about what the result is, and most managers aren't. They're very specific about what they want people to do, but they have no idea what that's going to achieve. People are smart and creative, and they bring that to the job if you create the space for them to do that.

We need two things in order to make a decision, we need information to base that decision on and we need the authority to feel it's my decision to make. The authority and information enable them to make the decisions that will achieve the results, because getting a result is not about actions, it's a series of decisions. The manager, the micro-manager will explain, "I want you to do this, then this, then this, then etc." They're almost standing over people step-by-step, to make sure they get it right, because fundamentally it's driven the manager's fear of failure.

They think, "If people don't follow the rituals that I've learned throughout my working life, then they might fail and then I've failed". Delegating is a series of controlled mistakes. It's giving people enough scope and authority that they can get things right. Then they feel good about it because they know it's them that did it. If they do mess it up a bit the smart manager protects against failure, significant failure, by increase the frequency of feedback, based on the challenge of the task.

If the task is very challenging, then what the manager might do is say, "Let's check in at the end of every day. Just five minutes, just to let me know how you're getting on, if you need any help from me."

They set the frequency of that feedback, but they allow the person to drive the feedback. If the manager says, "Oh, I wouldn't do it that like that. Oh no, you're better off doing that this way," immediately they're taking responsibility back. Immediately the person's going to think or say, "Well you do it then."

Any time the manager steps in and corrects, they're undoing all the good work that they've done. What they've got to do is set a frequency of feedback. We know we're going to have a conversation at five o'clock today and check in on how you're doing. Now that we've both agreed that, the person doing the task can drive that. "This is is how it's going. I'm a bit worried about this, what do you think I should do?" The manager might then say, "What do you think you could do?" They reply, "Well I was thinking about this." To which the smart manager says, "Great. Go and do it then and see what happens." Then the more confidence the person has in the task and the more confidence the manager has that they're going in the right direction, the more they can reduce the frequency of the feedback.

This is true in any self-correcting system. Cruise control in your car, central heating in your house, the faster the feedback, the faster the system will correct for errors. If the feedback is slow, the error will be bigger by the time the system notices there's an error, or a deviation. We increase the frequency of feedback, the system will self-correct, and now that learning belongs to the person doing the task, and they will bring innovations and ideas that the manager had been unaware of.

Now the manager can systemise that knowledge. They can say, "Well, you've done a great job on that. At the next team meeting, tell everybody what you did." They get a sense of achievement and you're sharing knowledge about best practice, which is continually evolving.

I think delegating, as an essential skill, it also takes care of staff development, because most of what people learn, they will learn from doing the job, but learning only comes from a process of reflection. Not just from doing it, but from the manager asking, "How did it go? What did you learn? What would you do differently next time?" Turning the performance of the task now into a reflective exercise, that completes the learning cycle. A two-minute conversation has turned an ordinary task into a tremendous learning experience.

Then the other thing it takes care of is succession planning. A company spends so much money trying to predict potential and doing psychometric profiles in assessment centres etc, to try and predict what somebody's potential is. Why? Just delegate to them, now they're working at a more challenging level of authority, delegate something to them and measure what they do. Don't try to guess whether they can do it or not, let them do it and see what happens.

What I see time and time again, when succession planning is based on prediction, they end up with a person who's been manoeuvred into and earmarked for a role goes to the interview and doesn't get it. The person who actually gets the job at the interview, which is the acid test, has come out of nowhere, and nobody expected that person to be able to demonstrate what they did, but they did. Why guess when we can test and measure?

What do you know now that you wish you knew when you were back in management?

I had a manager say to me recently that he wanted to improve his decision-making skills because he makes decisions too quickly, and then he ends up realising that he's made the wrong decision. He gave me this example. They had some big customer problem, the sales guy came to him explaining the situation, he made a decision about what to do about it, then it turned out to be the wrong decision, because later on, he found out some more information. I told him, "You made the right decision, based on the information that that sales guy wanted to give you. So that you would make the decision that he wanted you to make". He paused for a long time and he said, "Yeah, that's exactly what happened." The problem wasn't him being hasty, the problem was that information had been withheld deliberately, because the salesperson had a particular agenda and wanted him to do a certain thing.

I think everyone makes their own choice. As long as you're giving people all the information that's available, you're not responsible for the choices they make.

What's your one tip for the top?

Focus on the team, not the individuals. It's so easy for managers to get drawn into focusing on individuals. The noisiest bird in the nest gets the worm doesn't it?

It's easy for them to get distracted by individuals, either high performers or low performers, and they've got to work with this person, invest in them and coach them and so on. What they often don't notice is the impact that that has on the team. For example, if somebody's coming into work late and the manager doesn't do anything about that, other people in the team see that and they think "Well hang on, if they're getting away with it, why am I coming into work on time? I may as well not. Why am I putting myself out to do something that they're not doing?"

That sense of fairness, that innate sense of equity and fair treatment absolutely drives team cohesion and therefore team performance, so I think focus on the team, not the individuals, and do what's right for the team.

The individuals will come and go. I'm not a football fan, but if you're a football fan, you might think of your team now compared to your team 10 years, 20 years ago, it's still your favourite team, but the people who are in it are totally different, so you've got to focus on what maintains the integrity of the team, not on what's right or wrong for any individual in that.

I think let the team run the business. The manager runs the team, the team runs the business, and let them be responsible for that.

What's the one book you'd recommend everyone read.

I thought about management books, and I find often that they're one good idea that really could have been a LinkedIn article at best, padded out to be a book, because that's what sells. I've looked at it from a different angle, I would recommend Quirkology by Richard Wiseman.

Richard Wiseman is a psychology professor, and a lot of his research is into odd things about people and the odd things that people do. The subtitle of Quirkology is The Curious Science of Everyday Life.

Quirkology's great. It's just a collection of really interesting research into all kinds of weird things, scientifically working out what's the funniest joke in the world for example. It's interesting I think, because it shows you weird stuff about human behaviour, but approached from a scientific angle, and also described in a very engaging and interesting way. It's very readable.

Then also, anything by Raymond Chandler, the creator of Philip Marlowe, the detective.

Any of the Marlowe detective stories like Farewell my Lovely or The Big Sleep, or The Long Goodbye. He wrote short stories as well. The reason I'm recommending those rather than The One Minute Manager or serious management books is because they're tremendous observations of human behaviour and human motives.

I like the way that he creates this incredibly rich and vivid experience of the environment that these people are in as you're reading it, I think there are some useful lessons for leaders in terms of communication.

I also think reading books like that gives a different insight into human behaviour that I think is really fundamental to managers. I've talked about how everyone makes their own choice and that they have to live with the consequences of that choice. If people don't feel informed, then they don't necessarily feel good about the choices they make.

I think it just brings a different way of understanding human nature which is really fundamental to the job of a successful manager.

What's one question I haven't asked that you think I could have?

I did think about that and I thought maybe the question, 'What's the best thing about being a manager?'

Some people have said it's developing people, some say it's tackling strategic challenges. I think for me, it's about constantly developing myself. Learning more about people and human nature. Because the thing I found when I moved from working in the telecoms and IT industry into doing what I'm doing now, is that technical knowledge has a lifespan, and if you hang your career on technical knowledge, you're constantly having to update that, regardless of what industry that you work in.

It doesn't have to be IT, any industry is based on technical knowledge, law or HR for example, so you're constantly having to update that knowledge just to stay still.

Whereas I think knowledge about people, human behaviour and human nature, and organising people behind a task or a vision, that knowledge has no particular lifespan. What drives us as animals is much the same, I think the more you focus on acquiring and developing that sort of knowledge, the deeper it goes. I think that sort of abstract people knowledge is more valuable, more interesting for me.

Fundamentally, businesses 30 years ago were about machines, assets and land. Today, businesses are about flexibility, marketing, mind share and innovation and so on. Fundamentally, businesses will always be about people, so I think that's the thing I've enjoyed most. Simplifying and getting to the heart of what is it that gets people to do what they do. And therefore as a manager, how do I get them to do more of the things that are useful for the organisation?

What two things have struck you most from what was said?

What one thing will you do differently/employ as a result of what you've learnt from this chapter?

22

Peter Whent

Managing Director

Peter has directly launched or been part of the start-up team of three highly successful businesses, that were sold them for a combined total of a little over $100 million.

Today he helps startup entrepreneurs to launch their businesses and grow companies to scale up by avoiding all the pot holes he hit.

He is also a keynote speaker on human performance in business. He draws on his experience from active service in the Army, leading businesses, and as a Great Britain triathlete in his age group.

What was your greatest challenge as a middle manager?

I was always an entrepreneur at heart, so before I set up my first company, the biggest challenge for me was dealing with large company bureaucracy, politics and attitudes. People who felt it was more important to tick boxes and follow the handbook, then to get the job done well and quickly. People who were more concerned with covering their tracks, than serving our customers.

What was the biggest mistake you made when you were a middle manager?

It took me a while to learn that just because I was the boss, albeit of a small team, I didn't have to have all the answers. It takes a while to develop the maturity and confidence to understand your job is to marshal your troops to get the best result, not to do everything better than everyone yourself.

What personal qualities do you see in the best middle managers?

It's not a quality unique to middle managers; hard work. All the best performers I have worked with have a great work ethic. They understand that you get better by working hard at things. Almost without exception, they make a choice to be successful and they take full responsibility for it. There is no short cut and there's no substitute for effort. People who are relentless in their effort will always trump people who have more raw talent, but who don't apply themselves.

What do you know now that you wish you knew as a middle manager?

Patience! When you are at that level, you're in a hurry. But you come to learn that things change quicker than you think. Someone leaves, another company buys you, a big new customer comes in. Things can change almost daily. Don't despair.

What's your one Tip for the Top?

Don't spend your life thinking that everyone else knows better than you.

What is the one book you'd recommend to any and every middle manager?

Mindset by Dr Carol Dweck. It is the best book I have read about the mindset needed to achieve success, not just at work.

Who was the best boss you ever had and why?

A man named David Proctor. He bought my company and asked me to work for him. It was the best decision I made. He is the best manager of people I have ever seen. I learned a huge amount just by being around him and watching him in action. Over twenty years later we are still great friends.

What question haven't I asked that you think I should have?

What motivated you? Understanding your motivation and then finding a job that plays into that, is the way to make work happy, rewarding, fulfilling and successful. People who are personally motivated by their work can't wait to get out of bed in the morning.

What two things have struck you most from what was said?

What one thing will you do differently/employ as a result of what you've learnt from this chapter?

23

Phil Jones

Managing Director, Brother UK

What was your best memory or achievement as a middle manager?

Being exposed more to our European operation really opened up my eyes. I'd never been exposed to how business worked in different parts of the world including culture, etiquette, market dynamics and relationship building. It was a real calibration point in recognising how to get outcomes with competing priorities. I guess I remember this time as I seemed to quickly be able to develop rapport with people and find ways, regardless of barriers, to get consensus even if that sometimes meant difficulties for my own office. From this point, I think more started to happen for me as it built trust and strong relationships over time.

Who was the best boss you ever had and why?

A Japanese Managing Director – Hiroshi 'Harry' Suzuki. We had worked together previously when I was a young product manager and he was in charge of the major business unit back at our HQ in Japan. As a young subject matter expert, I recognised quickly that Harry always enquired about my opinion and took time to listen to my answers. He had great charisma combined with a phenomenal memory and ability to summarise which I learned a lot from. Later when he came to the UK to head up the business with myself as Sales Director, we made a great team. He taught me the value of bringing people with you and the power of influence over instruction.

What was the greatest challenge you faced as a middle manager?

When it got to the point that I was a manager of managers, not just a manager with a small line of direct reports. That was perhaps the time when I was challenged most to let go of the 'operational reigns' having to take a leadership role. When you've been in the detail a lot over a product and sales based career it's the equivalent of a bungee jump; having to let go of that need to know everything in detail. At first it's very difficult and you feel uncomfortable yet in the long term it's more effective to let others manager that detail and you join up the dots.

What was the biggest mistake you made when you were a middle manager?

Not spending enough time defining problems/opportunities. In a sales company there is a strong bias for action, sometimes like kids chasing a football searching for that glory goal. Task orientation is brilliant but make sure you don't end up working hard at something that doesn't get you what you want. Like the saying goes, some people are going nowhere fast!

By spending more time to define exactly what a problem was or what the opportunity is and really getting to the specifics, it's surprising how you can better co-ordinate your resources and get the most efficient outcome with an economy of effort. Einstein is reported to have said that if he only had one hour to solve a problem he would spend 55 minutes defining the problem and the remaining 5 minutes solving it. Lesson learned.

What personal qualities do you see in the best middle managers?

Looking across our people now it's those that have a blend of task orientation combined with an ability to motivate people. Motivation can be delivered in a variety of different ways, small notes, big gestures, verbal feedback or inspiration. Those that figure out the best way to get the best from their people get the best results in my experience.

What skills do you think middle managers should focus on developing to ensure their effectiveness over their career?

Mastery of self and mastery of subject matter. Really learn how you operate, what your default biases are, how your reactions work, how you think, react, view problems or deal with pressure. When you figure our what a complex being you really are, you will appreciate others. In terms of mastery of subject matter, always look to improve. Read books, spend time with peers, ask advice, go to conferences, stretch yourself.

What do you know now that you wish you knew as a middle manager?

Remove your mask. There's a pressure in the middle as you're keen to impress, stay in the lights and make your mark. That can often mean you end up being a revved up super manager, blasting through tasks, targets and teams leaving trails of destruction behind you as you look to confirm the decision taken to promote you. Be more situationally aware of those around you, what mask you put on when you walk through the door, what shadows you throw, what sunshine you strike. You'll learn later in your career or further up the ladder that the more authentic you are, the more you congruent you become, the happier you are and the better you lead.

What's your one Tip for the Top?

Build strong relationships in the business. Early in my sales career I figured out that spending time with operations colleagues from across the business could pay big dividends. Even if you don't have a specific overlap, it's worthwhile getting to know people, particularly in management and leadership positions as they can accelerate your learning, give relevant advice when needed and offer support to you as you advance up the career ladder.

What is the one book you'd recommend to every middle manager?

The Excellence Dividend by Tom Peters. Plain talking, no-nonsense blend of everything to do with strategy, people, quality thinking and pulling it all together.

What two things have struck you most from what was said?

What one thing will you do differently/employ as a result of what you've learnt from this chapter?

24

Review

Hi, it's Anthony, the book's author here.

How are you enjoying the book so far? If you have enjoyed it and it's given you some food for thought or some actionable things to do, could I ask you to leave a review on Amazon please?

Reviews are the oxygen for any book. My hope is that it can help many people navigate their careers and without enough reviews I just won't be able to do that.

What you say could make a difference to someone else's career.

Enjoy the rest of the book and see you at the end.

Best wishes,

Anthony

25

Shaun Wane

England Rugby League Head Coach, Business Owner, Speaker

Shaun Wane, was a professional rugby player for about 13 years. After a period of ten years working for Tarmac while coaching part time, he became Head Coach of Wigan Warriors RL from 2011 to 2018. During this time he won 3 Super League Grand Finals and two Challenge Cups.

He was also a high-performance coach with the Scottish Rugby Union, has his own construction company and is a regular keynote speaker about leadership and a winning mindset. He has just become Head Coach of England Rugby League.

What was your best memory or achievement when you were a manager with Tarmac?

I worked for many years for Tarmac and I worked under some senior managers who were very good, quite obsessive about winning and I learned a lot off them.

But what I've got gradually found out is that it's about looking at the detail and making people around me who worked with me, not necessarily for me, are performing by nailing the details.

People answering the phone in the office, answering the phone the best you can and being the most eloquent and well mannered. The cleaners doing their job really well, the people in the yard.

I didn't plan this to happen but it has developed in my personality. If you're going to do your job, no matter what it is, you do it the best you can. You're there eight, nine, ten hours a day and it's a long drag if your heart's not in it.

If you're heart's not in it get out and find something else. That was my belief. I had a really good team around me at Tarmac who all thought the same as me and that was to be the best, to be better than everybody else and sell more concrete.

To deliver better and if people wanted a quote other companies would take four days, I would take it back to them within an hour. Just to shock them into thinking they're different, they're better. My quotes had more detail and when we delivered kilos on site, my lads were well mannered because I coached them to be well mannered, it makes a difference, the small things all add up and make the difference.

When you look back on your business career then who was the best boss you've ever had and why?

I had two bosses, a guy called Albert Morley who was the director and a guy called Mike Bellamy who was my line manager, who was very, very impressive. Very supportive, very aggressive in the marketplace which is what I needed and looked after the detail, made sure that we were nailing the market here in Manchester.

What he taught me was the importance of detail. I always remember going into the meeting for the Hilton in Manchester, and seeing that the detail in our quote was far better than in other competitors. He was very aggressive, we won jobs and he rewarded well, he was just a very, good manager. A very good a man manager.

When things went wrong, which they did frequently back in that industry, he never panicked, he always stayed nice and calm and focused. One hundred percent of the time he would have been very, very worried, because we were talking hundreds of thousands of pounds sometimes. But he never showed it, he always stayed composed and smart. I learned a lot from him.

That served me well in rugby too. We've had some very, testing times off the field over the years at Wigan and I always remembered that lesson.

We had three years of an injury crisis like you can't imagine and my head of strength and conditioning come in my office with the physio and they were panicking, "We've no players and we'll have to get the kids in," they said.

Each time I was worried but I never showed them that. I just knew where we wanted to go, what we needed to do, what sort of attitude we needed from the young players and I made sure they understood it. And it worked out well, the young players did really well. I got all that off Mike. The best people in the world are the best thieves in the world, they pinch things off other people and develop it to be better for them.

What was the greatest challenge that you faced when you were in management?

Without going into the technicalities of concrete, things had to be on time to the minute. So it was about being very organised, and if something happened having a backup plan and anticipating what could go wrong and being prepared.

That's what happened with one particular job when two sites broke down, we couldn't supply a job and it was going to cost us a lot of money. So we had to make some tough decisions and let a few people down but we ended up getting it done. It was a case of damage limitation, we had to make some tough decisions and we did that.

But once you made them you just have to be tough with your convictions. You take all the advice off of all the educated people around you and then come up with a decision and once you do it, that's it, you stick with it and nothing can derail you.

It's been the same in sport too. I've had to make some very tough decisions. It might backfire, but as long as you know 100% you've listened to the right people, you've listened to the right amount of information and given it the due diligence, you come up with the decision. Once you make that decision whether it works out or not you've done the right thing, stick with it.

I've had some terrible stick off people about making certain decisions in rugby games, about team selections, but I'm adamant that I made the decision, I listened to the right people and I'm going to stick with it. Nothing will put me off that.

What are the personal qualities you see in the best managers?

Honesty. Being very honest, being brutally honest in a nice way, in a respectful way. The players who played for me at Wigan are my friends, we're really good friends, I go to their engagements, weddings and the kids christenings. I did all of that.

But when there were tough conversations needed about their form, and telling them they're not going to play, you can't back away from that. You need to be honest with your convictions, straightforward. Tell them straight between the eyes in a nice manner, but give them a way out. If I had to leave a player out for a very important game, a lot of the times players would drop themselves. What I mean by that is, I always give a lot of feedback and in business it's the same, I give daily, weekly feedback. I'd tell them what I was happy with about their game and what I wasn't.

I'd tell them; "If you keep doing this thing in defence it will give me reason to not play you." Then a week later is he doing it again. I'll watch his game again and we'll do things in training, me and him on our own, and I'll try and get him out of his bad habit and I'll do it.

After six weeks I'll get him in and I'll show him in detail and I'll ask him "What do you think." More often than not he would say: "Well I can't play, I should be dropped." So they would drop themselves.

But that's just honest, regular supportive feedback and make sure you're the one that works with them. You do it. I'm not easy to work for, I require the best for every meeting and training. You get regular feedback. So that is the key, honest, regular feedback. Some of the tough decisions I've had to make, such as leaving people out of cup final teams, never really bothered me.

At home my wife would say, "How could you drop so and so?" I'd reply, he's an absolutely fantastic player but he wasn't right for the World Club Challenge team. I had other people which could help us win that particular game."

At the end of the day the one thing that's going to help me and this team win this game, was an awkward conversation, but he understood because he's had regular feedback about his performance. My wife couldn't believe that I'd left him out because I was so friendly with him. But I knew it was the right thing, in that context friendship counts for nothing winning games is what matters. You just have to win the game no matter what, win at all costs. The player concerned understood and respected that.

I've got two girls and they're both working, they both have good jobs and buying houses. The other day my daughter was complaining about her solicitor, she's buying a house and her solicitor is slow and she gets into the detail, and I said to my daughter, "Phone him, text him, find out what's happening." She said, "I'll ring him tomorrow." I said, "No, no, pick up the phone up now and ring him."

Don't sleep on it, don't have another three hours thinking about it, deal with things now because stress and negative thoughts in your mind are not good. Get rid of it and deal with something else and move on and be more productive. So my kids understand it, I've learnt all my life about dealing with things straightaway, don't sit on them.

What skills do you think managers should focus on developing then to ensure their effectiveness over their career?

Being very supportive. I'm a family man. I love my family, I love my kids and being very supportive. If any player comes into me and says that they've got a parents evening or their kids need to go to the doctors, all my employees know that if they needed anything at all to do with their family they can have time off.

I'm very strict about that, about people having days off work with sickness and illness. I expect them to be very clean and look after their well being and make sure that they turn up for work every day, I don't like having people having time off work. I'm never ill and I don't expect my players to be ill and my work colleagues to be ill because they didn't look after themselves. We need to turn up and do our job every day.

But if a player has a problem with his family, with his wife, with his parents, they can as much time off as they want, I'll support them and they've got my trust until they lose it and they know that.

Having that trust and them understanding that you care for them, you're going to be brutal with them with their feedback about their game and about their performance at work. But when it's to do with family then you can have time off, we'll support you and them through the tough times.

Once that's gone and all your family's good and everybody's healthy you come into work and you do your absolute best at everything. I think you get it paid back in abundance when you need to.

It's not a case of "I've done this for you, you do that for me." It's a two-way thing. "I'll look after you, you look after your job and make sure I see the best in you every single day, every second you're doing your best."

What do you know now then that you wish you knew perhaps early on in your career?

I think I didn't start coaching young enough, I wish I'd gone into club coaching earlier because it's what I love doing, I enjoy it. I like the challenge of watching things and working out ways of winning. Everything happens for a reason I do believe that. I had a very good professional career, I enjoyed myself immensely. My life's been a good learning curve but coaching is what I enjoy and I just wish I could have had that from an earlier age.

What would be your one tip for the top?

Ask "What's next?" Never be happy. I had a very, very tough upbringing, I left home when I was 15 and I walked out my house, when my dad nearly killed me one day and I never went back, it left me homeless.

I was very naughty, a real tearaway. But after leaving I signed a professional contract a year later. I lived at my girlfriend's house and she's now my wife and I've always been the same; never been satisfied.

When we win games I'm never happy. I don't think I've ever been really happy with a game ever that I have coached at the top level. I know it sounds a bit strange that but don't be satisfied with things. There's always a way to be better. I remember when we played St Helens on an Easter Monday we beat them. We did a review of that game, ten minutes were positive and 20 minutes were negative about things we could do better.

So it's about never being happy. I've had some great jobs and I've always been fully engaged in my work, but I've always thought what is next?

I'm the same with both my daughters, we went away for New Year and went to Scotland with our dogs. Both my daughters are doing very well at work and I said to them round the table at night over a whiskey, "What's next for your both? What's your next role, where can you get a better salary, how are you going to improve yourself?"

That's what I'd say to any junior manager; never be happy, always find ways of improvement. I know a lot of people will disagree with that, but you asked me and that for me personally has been a big motivation for me. I'm 54 I'm in a great job I'm still thinking what's next? How can I improve what I do?

That's why I'm obsessed with watching two and three Scotland games a day, watching every single tackle and asking myself "How could they improve?" I'm watching a sport which I don't really know that well, but I am getting better and I'm coming up with stuff they they feel is useful. So that's very important for me, I need to be challenged and I need to push myself to get better.

If you had to recommend one book...

Leaders Eat Last, by Simon Sinek that's a great book.

What two things have struck you most from what was said?

What one thing will you do differently/employ as a result of what you've learnt from this chapter?

26

Stephen Hay

Management expert, adviser, speaker & author

Stephen specialises in working with middle managers for whom career change is not an option and who have no particular desire to join the ranks of the Executive Suite. He works to help them thrive within the corporate world rather than climb the ladder. He lives in New Zealand.

He works with managers who are motivated by doing the job of management well for its own sake. And helping their team members become excellent managers in their own right.

What is the greatest challenge facing middle managers?

There are several but I think the greatest challenge is the 3D pincer movement in which they find themselves on an almost daily basis:

- · from above, leadership directions that may not be clear or consistent
- · from below, staff reactions to those directions

- from left and right, peer pressure
- from the front, external programme and project managers driving change through the organisation
- from behind, a technical solution vendor.

What was the biggest mistake you've seen middle managers make?

Not recognising the multi-faceted challenge outlined above.

What personal qualities do you see in the best middle managers?

Patience. And a willingness to ask questions until the situation is clear, no matter who they are dealing with.

What skills do you think middle managers should focus on developing to ensure their effectiveness over their career?

Ensuring that everything they do helps to achieve someone else's objectives. Middle managers are first and foremost facilitators, facilitators of someone else's decisions. It's a fine art but one worth learning.

What's your one Tip for the Top?

Learn what your boss's boss's objectives are and make sure everything you say and do is framed in such a way that it shows that you are helping them meet their objectives. Your objectives are to help them meet theirs.

What is the one book you'd recommend to any and every middle manager?

I'll take a liberty and recommend two, actually, and they go hand-in-hand.

The first is "The Truth About Middle Managers" by Paul Osterman, MIT Sloan School of Management. He outlines the history of middle management, assesses the present (late 2000s) and then looks to the future. It is a powerful read and will help every middle manager situate themselves in the macro-level changes that are occurring in the business world.

The second could easily have been written specifically for middle managers. It is "The Effective Executive" by Peter Drucker. The first lines of the Preface bear repeating, "Management books usually deal with managing other people. The subject of this book is managing oneself for effectiveness." If there were one word to sum up middle management today it is that, effectiveness.

What two things have struck you most from what was said?

What one thing will you do differently/employ as a result of what you've learnt from this chapter?

27

Stuart Wallace

Executive Chairman, Prydis, Non-Executive Director
Hearts of Midlothian FC, former Partner at PwC

What was your best memory or achievement as a middle manager?

My greatest memory is working with some fabulous mentors, people who cared and really took an interest in my career. They helped me understand that I had the skills required to succeed in a highly competitive and complex organisation.

Who was the best boss you ever had and why?

The best 'boss' I ever had was our Regional Chairman at PwC in the Midlands. He helped me understand that there was life way beyond my specialist area, that my job was to deliver the whole of PwC to our clients. Essentially, he helped me develop into a much more rounded business professional than I would ever have been otherwise.

What was the greatest challenge you faced as a middle manager?

The business unit I was in was simply not large enough to support my aspirations. There was no clear pathway locally that would allow me to progress all the way through my firm, hence my biggest challenge was geography. I became somewhat nomadic, moving between Glasgow, Edinburgh, Aberdeen, Leicester and ultimately Birmingham. It was important I then set down roots to demonstrate that I could build and grow a business. My advice to others would be to look for the best opportunities wherever they might be, but to recognise that has to be carefully managed if you are also to succeed at home!

What was the biggest mistake you made when you were a middle manager?

As someone who did not graduate through University, for a long time I had an enormous chip on my shoulder and a lack of confidence in dealing with those individuals I worked with who were from the best Universities.

I was the only person holding me back. Ultimately, I turned that to my advantage by using it as an "I'll show you" type trigger. I also successfully navigated my professional exams at the ripe old age of 31, you're never too old to learn.

What personal qualities do you see in the best middle managers?

I always valued people with passion, hunger and integrity. Intellectual horsepower goes a long way, but without passion, hunger and drive there is a real danger it will be wasted. The best middle managers also have the ability to engage people more junior to them as well as people more senior to them in equal measure.

What skills do you think middle managers should focus on developing to ensure their effectiveness over their career?

Self-confidence, to recognise the skills they have which will allow them to progress.

Self-development, to recognise that those skills can always be enhanced and that those areas in need of development will add to their overall performance as they progress.

Self-awareness – recognise it is better to be respected than to be liked, but that you don't have to be a complete git in order to succeed!

What do you know now that you wish you knew as a middle manager?

That work life balance is more than just a cliche, not only is it possible to have balance and be successful, but that performance truly is enhanced in the workplace if you give yourself permission to spend quality time on what you love outside the workplace.

What's your one Tip for the Top?

You need strong sponsorship. Who is the one individual in your organisation that would truly die in a ditch for your success and progression?

What is the one book you'd recommend to every middle manager?

The good pub guide, you might need it....no seriously, Half The Sky: How to change the world. If you have a daughter, read this. If you want to know the direction of change in the workplace in the 21st century, read this.

What question haven't I asked that you think I should have?

Looking back, would you change any of the career choices you made?
    The answer has to be no, while there were mistakes, overall it's a clear no #noregrets.

What two things have struck you most from what was said?

What one thing will you do differently/employ as a result of what you've learnt from this chapter?

28

Ted Bell

CEO, Freddies Flowers

Ted started his working life as a graduate trainee with Unilever plc but after five fun years counting, marketing and selling soaps and deodorants, he switched career paths to become an investor working with 3i plc and then Close Brothers Private Equity. By his mid–thirties he decided he wanted to get involved in a business directly and was fortunate enough to join Abel & Cole as FD just as the organic retailer was taking off. Over the next eight years, Ted graduated from FD to MD, completed a buyout of the business in Oct 2007, followed by a refinancing in Feb 2010 and finally a trade sale in Oct 2012.

In 2015 Ted joined a former colleague who had just started his own flower business, Freddie's Flowers. Since starting just over three years ago, they have taken the business from a back garden to a business with 30,000 customers nationwide and profitable sales of over £10m pa.

What was the greatest challenge you faced as a middle manager?

Persuading an investment committee to support my recommended acquisitions. It took me a long time to realise that, in addition to good judgement and rigorous diligence, it was vital to demonstrate great confidence. I was also slow to identify how often the key decision was made well before the formal investment committee meeting took place. Lobbying support with key decision makers beforehand was vital.

Who was the best boss you ever had and why?

Keith Abel, the founder of Abel & Cole, was perhaps my best boss. Together (he as CEO and me as FD) we steered the business through a very tricky restructuring and into growth. Our skills complimented each other well and throughout our time working together he consistently trusted me. He was also very happy and quick to hand over the reins once I was ready to take over.

What was the biggest mistake you made when you were a middle manager?

Assuming that people in more senior positions always know better.

What personal qualities do you see in the best middle managers?

Intelligence and commitment are important but, for me, what really marks out the best middle managers is independence of thought, common sense and an ability just to get things done.

What skills do you think middle managers should focus on developing to ensure their effectiveness over their career?

Communication, planning and delegation.

A good manager's key contribution is to make other people more productive. To achieve this you must make your team genuinely believe their success is your primary goal.

What do you know now that you wish you knew as a middle manager?

Common sense seems to be incredibly rare. It ought to be called 'rare sense'.

What's your one Tip for the Top?

Take a risk and back yourself.

What is the one book you'd recommend to every middle manager?

Anything by Wilbur Smith – relax in the evenings.

What two things have struck you most from what was said?

What one thing will you do differently/employ as a result of what you've learnt from this chapter?

29

Tim Lock

Managing Director, NewLaw Solicitors

A Chartered Accountant with 19 years' experience operating at board level within fast growing medium and large companies as both CFO/FD and Commercial Director.

Co-founder and FD of Co-operative Legal Services (CLS), one of the UK's first Alternative Business Structure legal practices. CLS grew from 4 employees to 550 in six years and was valued at £60m in 2012 at disposal.

Tim is now Managing Director of NewLaw Solicitors, a leading UK law firm specialising in running Solicitor Practices for major UK brands.

What was the greatest challenge you faced as a middle manager?

I am incredibly fortunate that I was only a middle manager for a short period of time. From qualifying as a Chartered Accountant to being made CFO of a multi-million dollar company was only a year. This was in the early days of the internet boom and I was in the right place at the right time and someone took a chance on me.

During my brief stint in middle management the biggest challenge was being asked to do things you don't believe in and fundamentally don't think were right. I have had a couple of moments like this and I stuck to my guns even when one time it meant deciding to move on.

It turned out to be a great decision, and led to a big opportunity.

What was the biggest mistake you made when you were a middle manager?

I once criticised a more senior colleague to his boss and got a real dressing down. I wanted the floor to swallow me up but instead I had to sit and take it on the chin.

That taught me that keeping your own counsel at times can be as important as what you have to say, and avoid office politics as much as you can!

What personal qualities do you see in the best middle managers?

The best middle managers I have worked with give you the sense that they have everything under control. They do this through organisation, planning and hard work. Hard work doesn't mean long hours, it means working quickly and effectively when they are at work. In my experience you get a lot more from someone who has a fulfilled personal life than someone who does an 80 hour week. Great middle managers also focus on improvement and mentoring of their staff as a priority.

What skills do you think middle managers should focus on developing to ensure their effectiveness over their career?

Communication is key. My Mum ran a hairdressing business out of our house when I was a boy and I've often said that what I learned about speaking to people from all walks of life during that time has helped me as much as any education or training I've ever had.

This has translated into being able to have difficult conversations. When you manage people your success is based on their success, but many of us would rather retreat to our email inbox or a nice spreadsheet rather than go and have a conversation with someone about what they are struggling with in their role and how you can help them overcome the problems.

Finally, don't sit on bad news. If you face a difficultly share it early before it becomes big bad news!

What do you know now that you wish you knew as a middle manager?

Don't be afraid to take risks with your career. Often a change is as good as a promotion and you can often move up quicker by moving business than by staying put. Oh, and never get involved in email arguments!

What's your one Tip for the Top?

I've not tried this myself but I worked with someone once who had a trick of making a big show of getting up and making a coffee at 5.30pm as people were starting to leave. This gave the impression he was in for a late finish. 15 minutes later when 75% of the office was empty he would leave. It worked, he was promoted to Senior Manager quicker than any of his peer group!

What is the one book you'd recommend to any and every middle manager?

I have to confess I don't read a lot of business books, I'd rather read a good thriller. I do however enjoy books that focus on what makes people elite at anything, and the best book I've read on that is Malcolm Gladwell's Outliers. I certainly have benefited from one of his central theories that opportunity, or "right place at the right time" is a big ingredient to success.

Who was the best boss you ever had and why?

I believe a great boss needs to show that they trust you, and Eddie Ryan, who I worked with across three businesses in total, always placed a huge amount of faith in me and my abilities. He also did something which has become a bit out of fashion, he led. Eddie made decisions and stuck with them, which I believe is vital in business.

What two things have struck you most from what was said?

What one thing will you do differently/employ as a result of what you learnt in this chapter?

30

Tina O'Brien

Managing Director, Exactech

Tina started her career as a registered nurse and in the late '80s she decided to pursue a commercial career as a sales representative in medical sales. She loved the fast paced environment and her ambition and experience took her into sales management and eventually into senior management positions. She worked for three companies before setting up and becoming Managing Director with Exactech, who provide shoulder replacements and associated products to the NHS and private sector.

What was the greatest challenge you faced as a middle manager?

Keeping the whole team motivated when product supply was an issue. I did this by having the team working together and putting pressure on manufacturing to ensure the product was supplied in a timely manor.

What was the biggest mistake you made when you were a middle manager?

Trying to please everyone all of the time. Worrying too much about what people thought rather than having the confidence that I was doing the right thing

What personal qualities do you see in the best middle managers?

Good leadership skills, leading from the front. Being in the field with the team and gaining relationships with customers. It's important to have the team on your side and supporting management rather than creating a them and us situation. It is important as a middle manager to have a seamless link between the team and senior management.

What skills do you think middle managers should focus on developing to ensure their effectiveness over their career?

Keeping up with the change in generations and using a more of a coaching approach rather than the old autocratic approach.

What do you know now that you wish you knew as a middle manager?

I can't please everyone all of the time, but I can deliver bad news by turning things into a positive, no matter how challenging they are.

What's your one Tip for the Top?

Have confidence in what you are doing and listen to team members ideas no matter how junior they are.

What is the one book you'd recommend to any and every middle manager?

Our Iceberg is Melting – John Kotter

Who was the best boss you ever had and why?

The Managing Director of the Company I was the Global Business Director at. He always kept calm in the most stressful situations and helped us through the challenging time

What question haven't I asked that you think I should have?

What keeps you going?
   The Buzz

What two things have struck you most from what was said?

What one thing will you do differently/employ as a result of what you've learnt from this chapter?

31

The Six ATONS for career success

Congratulations if you made it all the way here having read every chapter. What did you learn?

That's what really matters isn't it? What each of us takes from the book will differ for a whole bunch of reasons. It will be intensely personal because where you are at and where you have come from is unique to you, and only you know where you want to go.

What I have come up with is what I think are the six key things that every manager who aspires to either make it to the top, or just be the best they can be, should focus on doing. These are based on an analysis of what each contributor had to say.

I've called them the 'six ATONS'. In nautical terms an ATON is 'an aid to navigation'. By using these aids I believe you'll be better equipped to navigate your way though your career to whatever destination you choose.

These are:

1. Delegate
2. Accept the hierarchy
3. Master thyself
4. Develop the mental fitness to lead
5. Influence not instruct

6. Get a sponsor/mentor

Delegate

The ability to delegate effectively was frequently one of the most talked about abilities whether directly or indirectly. Teaching his officers to delegate effectively was one of the ways that L. David Marquet turned the nuclear powered submarine, the Sante Fe from one of the worst in the US Navy to one of the best.

He said: "We had no need for leadership development programmes, the way we ran the ship was the leadership development programme. It was one of the mechanisms I credit for the significantly disproportionate number of promotions issued among Santa Fe's officers over the last decade".

Peter Freeth's chapter and his AIR framework provide an excellent insight into the whole subject of delegation, what stops mangers doing it and how to get better at it. If you skipped that then think about going back and reading it.

Accept the Hierarchy

In hindsight, this is where I went wrong on my career. It's also what Darcy Willson-Rymer talked about in his chapter, "One other thing I would say is subscribe to the hierarchy. The hierarchy always needs to be company first, function second, self-third.

You always need to put the mission of the enterprise ahead of your own personal mission. Or that of your function."

Harvey Coleman in his book, Empowering Yourself - The Organisation Game Revealed said, "You can be a team player or you can be a distraction," and "whoever is at the top of the pyramid has the right (and obligation) to make the rules."

I found it increasingly difficult to do that when I didn't believe in the purpose of the organisation or the people leading me. And therein lies the challenge for managers. How can you inspire the people you lead so that it becomes easy for them to subscribe to the hierarchy? Ultimately, of course, it comes down to a personal decision from each one of us. Do we subscribe or not? If not you should move on and not become "a distraction" and find an organisation where you can accept the hierarchy because that will save you a lot of frustration and unhappiness.

Master thyself

Emotional intelligence is a golden thread that runs through almost every single one of the contributions. Made popular by Daniel Goleman's work in the 1990s its a fundamental requisite for anyone wanting to lead effectively and make it to the top.

Dr. Goleman described emotional intelligence as a person's ability to manage his feelings so that those feelings are expressed appropriately and effectively. According to Goleman, emotional intelligence is the largest single predictor of success in the workplace.

Perhaps it is the founder of the Stoic philosophy, Epictetus, who said it best, "No man is free who is not master of himself".

Mastering ourselves by developing our emotional intelligence is a life-long journey where even a short-term slip can have long lasting consequences. The positive pay-offs though can be life-enhancing.

Develop the mental fitness to lead

I've used the term mental fitness over mental toughness deliberately. Mental toughness is one of the most important, yet often misunderstood concepts in leadership. It is our ability to handle stress, pressure and challenge irrespective of the prevailing circumstances.

However, to be truly effective it needs to be applied with a large dose of emotional intelligence and I think, increasingly, an awareness of mental health. In my opinion the truly effective, modern leader will need and lead with a deep appreciation of and for all three, hence the term mental fitness.

High levels of mental toughness without emotional intelligence is akin to driving a high power sports car on ice with normal tyres; you'll just spin your wheels and slide off the road. The modern leader also has to have an understanding of mental health, how to look after their own and the people they lead. We all have a responsibility to shift the needle away from stigma and discrimination to enlightenment and understanding. Even if it's for selfish reasons. After all, poor mental health will affect 1 in 4 people every year. Can you be so sure it won't be you? Or someone you love.

Influence not instruct

Much has been said and written by many great thinkers about the changing nature of society and leadership away from the top down command and control popular through much of human history. It is said that millennials want to be led differently than previous generations. I don't think they do. I think most people always wanted to be led or engaged that way, it's just that society didn't know anything different. There's nothing special about millennials per se (sorry millennals but there isn't) it's just that societal thinking and expectations have incrementally changed over time. Thank goodness too.

Brigadier John Thomson talked about it in his section, where even in the military there is a subtle change happening. He uses the example of General Stan McChrystal and his book, Team of Teams to make the point. Commander L. David Marquet also talked about it in his book that I mentioned earlier.

It's one of the reasons why coaching has seen an explosion in popularity over the last 20 years or more. Effective leaders influence not instruct.

Get a sponsor/mentor

Every single person interviewed for the book talked about having a sponsor or mentor who had a significant impact on their career. Whether it was Damian Hughes with Bernard Counsell, or Gary Kibble with Mark Newton-Jones everyone has benefited from some kind of mentor.

Harvey Coleman says in his book, "the ability to move up to the next level is dependent upon securing a sponsor who will pull that person to the next level".

Having interviewed all these people it seems to me that without someone to help 'pull you up' the chances of making it to the top are slimmer. In fact isn't a mentor the best representation of an ATON?

Who can you ask to be your mentor?

It was Epictetus who said, "One that desires to excel, should endeavour in those things that are themselves most excellent." If you choose to excel at each of those five ATONS and get yourself a worthy mentor, then I firmly believe you will excel in your career, whatever that looks like for you.

Afterword

What kind of legacy do you want to leave?

Blake Jamieson, an artist who paints pop art portraits of famous tech and sports heroes reminds us that: "Building a personal brand is much bigger than building a business. The only exit strategy is legacy."

Whatever career heights you scale or aspire to scale is not really important at the end of the day. I believe what matters most is the legacy we leave behind. Our legacy, to me, becomes not how much we earn't, what title we acquired or what size of business we grew, but what people say about us when we aren't around anymore.

My aim with this book, actually wasn't to help you get to the top necessarily. It was to help you be the kind of leader people want to follow on your journey, to talk about fondly about years after you no longer work together. The kind of person that made a positive difference to other people's lives and careers.

I hope you feel you are better equipped now to take that journey and leave a legacy your family, friends and colleagues will be proud to talk about while at the same time achieving your career goals.

Our time together has come to a close, so I'd just like to leave you with a quote from a man who did just that.

"The most powerful leadership tool we have, is our own example," John Wooden.

Recommended Books

The following list is of the books recommended by the contributors. And a couple of my own! I've ranked them by their Amazon sales numbers. Not perhaps the most scientific, but the most simple!

1. Chimp Paradox, Steve Peters https://amzn.to/39hJm7C
2. Mindset, Carol Dweck https://amzn.to/2TjPcj8
3. Start with Why, Simon Sinek https://amzn.to/3apsVWY
4. The Seven Habits of Highly Effective People, Stephen Covey https://amzn.to/3cqH2wN
5. Outliers, Malcolm Gladwell https://amzn.to/38leBgF
6. Leaders Eat Last, Simon Sinek https://amzn.to/2IhkWze
7. The One Minute Manager, Ken Blanchard https://amzn.to/39q83Pm
8. Team of Teams, General Stanley McChrystal https://amzn.to/2K9y5el
9. The Leopard Hunts in the Darkness, Wilbur Smith https://amzn.to/39q83Pm
10. Our Iceberg is Melting, John Kotter https://amzn.to/2woUvF7
11. Crucial Conversations, Kerry Paterson & Joeseph Grenny https://amzn.to/2vD33In
12. Gravitas, Caroline Goyder https://amzn.to/2IfHKiK
13. Turn the Ship Around, L. David Marquet https://amzn.to/3cbgw9Q
14. Endurance, Alfred Lansing https://amzn.to/2VJN1qH
15. Half the Sky – How to change the World, https://amzn.to/2TiMQ49
16. Key Concepts, Pierre Bordieu https://amzn.to/32Kc6mU
17. The Excellence Dividend, Tom Peters https://amzn.to/2IbLH8d

18. Liquid Thinking, Damien Hughes https://amzn.to/2TyBW9h

19. Servant Leadership, Robert Greenleaf https://amzn.to/38hMAXh

20. Survival of the Savvy, Rick Brandon, https://amzn.to/2PIafd3

21. Leadership Laid Bare, Graham Wilson https://amzn.to/32ITBPQ

22. The Power of Character, Andrew Reay https://amzn.to/2IdMFR4

23. Quirkology, Richard Wiseman https://amzn.to/3akPIDh

24. The Truth About Middle Managers, Paul Osterman https://amzn.to/38ldWvH

25. Consiglieri, Richard Hytner https://amzn.to/2wtYWyb

26. Empowering yourself: the organisational game revealed, Harvey Coleman https://amzn.to/3e7rkb5

27. Maverick! Ricardo Semler https://amzn.to/3ekLcYe

About the Author

Anthony runs ThreeFifty9, a mental skills speaking and training consultancy, that specialises in equipping people and teams with the mental skills needed to thrive in today's world. We focus on developing personal and leadership performance through mental fitness - the application of mental toughness and emotional intelligence combined.

Anthony brings the experience of a 20-year career across the private and public sector both nationally and internationally.

He held several Head of Communications positions in both public and private sector organisations and built a successful publishing company in the Caribbean.

Anthony has been coaching since 2006 and has chosen to work predominantly with middle management.

Over the last five years Anthony has worked with clients across numerous sectors including social housing, professional services, automotive, public sector, armed forces, retail, construction, energy and technology. These include: KPMG, AO.com, Veolia, Royal Navy, Goldman Sachs and WH Smith to name a few.

You can contact him at: anthony@threefifty9.com or via any of the methods below.

You can connect with me on:

🜨 https://www.threefifty9.com

🐦 https://twitter.com/AntTaylor72

🔗 https://www.linkedin.com/in/anthonytaylor-mentalfitness

Subscribe to my newsletter:

✉ https://sendfox.com/anthony

Also by Anthony Taylor

Anthony has also written a guide book to where he lived in the Caribbean. He is currently working on three other books: The 60min Guide to Personal Resilience, Mental Toughness Metaphors and The Untroubled Mind. Sign up to his email list to receive updates and free chapters as these books progress.

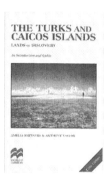

Turks & Caicos: Lands of Discovery (Macmillan)

This 3rd edition of the ever popular guidebook has been fully updated to reflect the changes in visitor destinations from Grand Turk to Provo, while retaining the insight into the culture and history often overlooked in other guidebooks that combine TCI with The Bahamas.

Printed in Poland
by Amazon Fulfillment
Poland Sp. z o.o., Wrocław

58594541R00132